Twelve Handkerchiefs

"Lest you should have shame for the place where you were born, these exquisite examples of an exquisite art will, I hope, enable you to bear yourself bravely against all contumely of ignorant people."
—Cecil Herbert Wood
June 3, 1939

Twelve Handkerchiefs

The global journey of Alice Wood Bulkeley
through World War II and the twentieth
century with an American Navy hero.

Joan Bulkeley Stade

With best wishes,

Joan Bulkeley Stade
USS Bulkley DDG-84

Sponsor

The Patrice Press ⟚ Tucson, Arizona

For more information on John Bulkeley and the USS *Bulkeley,* please visit
www.ussbulkeley.com or www.spear.navy.mil/ships/ddg84

THE PATRICE PRESS
Box 85639 / Tucson, AZ 85754-5639
1/800/367/9242
Email: books@patricepress.com
www.patricepress.com

Dedication

To my mother, Alice Wood Bulkeley, who has always been the anchor of our family. She is the voice of this story and our family treasure.

To my husband, Herbert Stade; my daughter and son-in-law, Karen and Scott Krill; my daughter Sharon Stade and son-in-law Tom Hense; our grandchildren, Samantha and Tyler Krill; my sisters Gina Bulkeley Day and Diana Bulkeley Lindsay; and my brothers, John D. Bulkeley, Jr. and Peter Wood Bulkeley.

And to Dad and to Peter Tare Bulkeley, who are already home with God in His loving care.

All of you have blessed and enriched my life's journey with so much love,

—Joan Bulkeley Stade

Acknowledgments

For many years, I have thought about telling my mother's remarkable story. I felt it deserved and needed to be told.

Numerous books have been written about my father's exploits and heroism during World War II. In 1945, MGM premiered the film *They Were Expendable*, depicting his command of Motor Torpedo Boat Squadron 3, which was relentlessly attacked in the Philippines just after that fateful Sunday morning at Pearl Harbor.

But Mother's birth and her early years in China continued to fascinate me. Her family had endured unspeakable suffering, hardships, and horror when they were captives of the Imperial Japanese Army.

My father saved my mother and brought her here to America. Together, they raised a family with love and pride.

So I am especially grateful to Mother, one of God's angels on Earth, for her interviews, letters, diaries, and photographs; to my Aunt Leilah Wood, Uncle Eric Wood, and cousin Allana Arnot, for all of their assistance; to Frances and Jeffrey Kraft, who worked with me as a team to archive, research, and provide early drafts of many chapters; my brother, Captain Peter Wood Bulkeley, USN (Ret.); my sisters, Gina Bulkeley Day and Diana Bulkeley Lindsay; and my niece, Kelley Alice Lindsay, for their invaluable assistance with this project and dream of mine.

This story has helped all of us to better understand and to more fully appreciate, with tremendous admiration, Alice Wood Bulkeley and the men and women who have been an inspiration to us and who have, in recent years, become known as The Greatest Generation. I hope that this book conveys at least a part of all that this generation sacrificed and endured.

—Joan Bulkeley Stade
November 10, 2001

Contents

Two Months in Turmoil

CHAPTER ONE
1942

Faith has been my anchor.
Alice Wood Bulkeley

Alice and John meet at New York's LaGuardia airport May 8, 1942,
after his daring rescue of General MacArthur in the Philippines.

On March 11, 1942, the world changed for Alice Wood Bulkeley, but she wasn't even present at the event that would throw her life into the middle of the public eye.

Just off the Philippine island of Corregidor, her husband, Navy Lieutenant John Duncan Bulkeley, had broken through a Japanese blockade on the 77-foot motor torpedo boat, *PT-41*, to whisk to safety Gen. Douglas MacArthur, his wife, young son, and key staff members to Australia under cover of darkness.

At home in Long Island City, New York, and almost nine months into her second pregnancy, Alice waited for any news that might come from her husband. He had always been a consistent letter writer, but she hadn't heard from him since Pearl Harbor was bombed back in December. Other news trickled in over the radio as she sat anxiously with her mother-in-law, Elizabeth MacCuaig Bulkeley and Elizabeth's sister Isabel, who both shared the four-room apartment with Alice and her eighteen-month-old daughter Joan. Alice's nights were spent serving as a civil defense air raid warden of New York's Sector D, Post 9, and studying for classes she was taking at a local college.

On March 23, Alice received a call that made her heart stop. For a moment she thought it was the call she had feared for months—one bringing her news that her husband, previously reported missing in action, was dead somewhere in the Pacific. But it was a reporter for the *Long Island Star* calling to ask how she felt about her husband's extraordinary heroism. It was electrifying news. As he filled her in on the details, she became numb with astonishment and happiness.

Almost immediately, an avalanche of attention came her way. Reporters were calling endlessly, asking for interviews. After a period of being overwhelmed with media appearances, the navy finally sent a full-time public relations officer to help Alice keep the newsmen at bay.

In addition to dealing with John's sudden fame and not knowing his whereabouts, Alice was consumed with worry over the fate of her family back in China. She had been raised in China, the daughter of a British father and Japanese/German mother. Although she considered herself a British subject, her "Eurasian" blood had been a constant issue throughout her childhood. Now with newsmen prodding for every detail of the famous hero and his beautiful wife, she feared the nation would learn that she carried the blood of America's two most hated enemies.

Through sketchy reports, she knew that her mother, two sisters, brother-in-law, niece, and nephew were held at Camp Stanley in Japanese-occupied Hong Kong as prisoners. Her younger brother was in a prison camp in Osaka, Japan, and her father was in a prison camp in Shanghai. She had not received word from them in months and feared the worst.

On the night of April 3, Alice went into labor. It was

arduous from the start—a second breech birth for her. In the delivery room of the Brooklyn Naval Hospital, Dr. Heinlein and his nurses gave Alice all the help and comfort they could. During the delivery, high forceps were used and the baby lacked oxygen. Suddenly Alice heard the doctor exclaim in a horrified voice, "Oh my God!" She was immediately anesthetized and had little time to contemplate the situation before she was asleep. She would remain asleep until the following evening.

When two doctors approached her bed, they informed her that her baby was alive, but that he had serious deformities and they could not give her a prognosis. Isabel MacCuaig, John's aunt, who was an obstetrical nurse, was in the room. Looking at her face, Alice knew immediately that she had seen the baby. It was a little boy—just what Alice and John had hoped for and referred to as "Oscar" for so many months. Alice just wanted to see him.

He was of good size. His body was perfectly formed except for a clubfoot and a webbed hand. His eyes were badly crossed and damaged. He could only whimper and his face was partially paralyzed. Later they would discover that he suffered from cerebral palsy. Alice could see that there was already a sort of determination in this little child to live. He was a fighter like his father and, because she wasn't sure John would make it home alive, she named him after her husband. Her first thought was to ask God to take him so he wouldn't live to suffer. Her second thought was of the newsmen who were waiting to see the baby.

After a week in the hospital, Alice took the baby home, ready to face a life that would now include one more enormous challenge. The next month was spent taking care of

Johnny's needs and those of Joan, who was not yet two years old. Isabel and Elizabeth, who was a surgical nurse, helped enormously, not only with medical care, but also with developing ways to wrap him in a blanket so that newsmen wouldn't see all of his physical deformities. Thankfully Joan was a beautiful, charismatic child who was a perfect foil for the media's attention.

May 7, 1942, brought a call from the navy that John and three other PT boat officers had arrived in San Francisco. Later that day Alice's navy contact brought a wire photograph of the group upon their arrival. The news media were again at her door. She didn't let on that she knew the date and time of their arrival. As it turned out, she didn't need to. The media had followed her every move.

Alice had been informed that John would be landing at New York's LaGuardia airport at 9 A.M. on May 8. With emotions that ran between elation and despair, she spent some of her last savings from her job as a confidential secretary at Butterfield & Swire in China to purchase clothes suitable for a hero's wife. Until now, her time in New York had been spent in the same clothes that had made the trip from China along with bed, bath, and table linens in eight ornately carved wooden chests. She pulled on a pair of white gloves, smoothed out the fitted polka-dot dress with the white collar, and positioned her new feathered hat elegantly on her head. From her top dresser drawer she gently took out an intricately embroidered handkerchief and put it in her pocketbook. Although she had given birth barely a month earlier, she was a slim—almost fragile—silhouette.

While Elizabeth stayed home with the children, Alice

raced to LaGuardia with John's father, Frederick, hoping to have a private reunion with John. It was not to be. As they approached the airport, they saw hundreds of people ten rows deep, including reporters, waiting to catch a glimpse of one of America's earliest World War II heroes.

Alice's mind was in a bit of a turmoil. Naturally, she was happy to welcome her husband home and thankful he was all in one piece, though a little thinner than when she had last seen him. He had, in fact, lost thirty pounds. But the thought of him meeting his new son preyed on her mind. She felt that she had failed her "darling" as she always called him. He was a sensitive, proud and private person. Here he was suddenly loved and admired by the whole nation and she was about to deliver news that would take all the joy out of this moment. John had been through enough disaster, Alice thought. It was not fair. Somehow she had to prepare him to meet his son.

The United Airlines Mainliner touched down at 10:22. By this time, the newsmen had surrounded them. They were calling for a picture of the couple embracing. As they leaned in toward each other, Alice began to whisper the words she had practiced in her mind for days: "Everything is not OK with the baby." But John jumped in first: "You sure are a long way from Kialat Road in Swatow."

Cecil and Emily

CHAPTER TWO
1880-1912

Material things can be replaced but what really
matters is your health and your life.

Emily Wood

Emily Ritsu Umetsu (pictured at the time of her wedding) and
Cecil Herbert Wood came from two very different backgrounds.

The young couple knew, when they saw the dark, turbulent waves coming in the wake of a late-season typhoon, that they would have to abandon their plan. They had intended for the birth of their second child to take place in the British crown colony of Hong Kong. Both wanted the baby born on British soil and duly registered as a British subject, just as they had done with their first child. But the ferry that was to take them down the China coast was nowhere to be seen. Cecil Wood escorted his petite wife, Emily, from the windswept harborfront across to the Astor House Hotel, the only European hotel in the port city of Swatow.

Both Cecil and Emily had become accustomed to the changes in plans that had to be made when one lived, as they did, in a colonial outpost, even though it was in the second largest city in the Chinese province of Guangdong. And that day at the Astor House, they would have to make yet another accommodation. No doctors were available. Cecil promptly rolled up his sleeves and assisted in the delivery of his second child and second daughter, a healthy, six-pound girl who they named Hilda Alice, but who would be called simply Alice.

It was November 19, 1912. Alice had entered the world

on foreign soil, amid stormy seas, with the help of the hands-on, can-do, self-made man that was her father. In many ways, Alice would become a child of the sea, and her father was the man who inspired it.

. . . .

Cecil Herbert Wood was born into comfortable circumstances in the Hyde Park district of London on March 15, 1880, the second of five children born to Dr. Henry Thorold Wood and his wife, the former Alice White of Eastborne, Sussex. A delightful child with blond hair, Cecil's family nicknamed him "Sunshine."

Dr. Wood was a member of the Royal College of Surgeons, served the royal family and had written a book on chest surgery. From this, one might surmise that Cecil should have become a stiff, detached, and analytical Victorian. But, as the second son, he was less pressured than his elder brother to enter the family business. Family rumor has it that while grudgingly studying for a medical career he blew up a laboratory, embarrassing his father and putting to an end for good the possibility of a career that he didn't want in the first place. Since it was assumed his father's fortune would go directly to his oldest brother, as was customary, Cecil and the younger brothers set out to distant corners of the world—Canada and China.

Boyhood holidays spent in the seaport of Eastbourne cultivated a love of the sea. Cecil completed his training there as a merchant marine. His brother Montagu saw him off, and Cecil worked as a cabin boy, eventually arriving in one of the most beautiful harbors in the world— Hong Kong. He was abandoning his home soil in Queen Victoria's England to make his fortune within the wide geography of a world full of Union Jacks, "upon which the sun never set." Over time, he worked his way up the ranks to the status of captain. Although he was engaged to a British girl back home before leaving for the Far East, she gave up on him when Cecil fell from the mast of his ship, receiving a concussion, and failed to write her for a lengthy period of time. She subsequently became an Episcopal nun.

In 1910, Cecil purchased shares in the South China Pilotage Association and moved to Swatow to become its junior port pilot in the employ of Lloyd's of London. In this capacity, he was responsible for escorting both the merchant ships and later the warships (which most commonly flew British, American, or Japanese flags), through the complex Swatow harbor. A man of two continents, Captain Wood readily applied the lessons learned in his homeland amid the overwhelmingly foreign circumstances in which he found himself. He became accustomed to the lush tropical landscape of South China, with its accompanying oppressive heat and humidity. He performed his duties resourcefully and efficiently by imposing the discipline and educational principles that he had come to respect from the damp, cold, and ordered world that he had left behind as a headstrong young man.

Cecil stood nearly six feet tall, an almost overpowering height in the early twentieth century. This fact, combined with his fair hair and skin and brilliant blue eyes, made him unmistakably Anglo-Saxon, especially when set against the colorful crush of Hong Kong's indigenous and various foreign populations. He was surrounded by, and moved within, an entire community of expatriates, many but not all of whom were British.

.   .   .   .

Emily Ritsu Umetsu was born worlds apart from Cecil Wood in the tiny fishing village of Shimabara, near Nagasaki, Japan, on August 15, 1889. In 1638, this village had been the site of a religious uprising during which as many as 30,000 people, most of them Christians, were slaughtered by the Japanese government forces. This put an end to open Christian worship for two centuries. Emily's father was Erich Von Maline, a German merchant seeking his fortune in the Far East. Sami Umetsu, her Japanese mother, had a passionate but brief love affair with him at a time when such intercultural liaisons were unfathomable within any society, let alone among the Japanese. Erich departed Japan without knowing that Sami was with child, and Sami never saw nor heard from him again. Emily would carry his photograph with her for the rest of her life.

Called by her given name of Ritsu (she wouldn't adopt the English name "Emily" until later) Emily was raised by Sami's grandparents in Shimonoseki, a fishing village located further to the north, on Kyushi Island. Her grandparents were loving and good to her, and Emily enjoyed a happy early childhood. Her tall grandfather was well educated and a devout Buddhist, and she would tag along with him to ring the bells at the temple and say the prayer beads. Discrimination only caused her discomfort when she was of school age. She was later educated by missionaries, learning a little English in Nagasaki. Her mother continued to work as a nurse in the employ of an American doctor, Dr. Newman, who cared enough for her to offer marriage and to adopt and educate Emily in America.

It was not to be. In 1903, Dr. Newman died and was buried in Nagasaki.

Sami moved to Hong Kong to seek better employment opportunities, leaving Emily with her grandparents. In 1906, when Emily was sixteen, she joined her mother in Hong Kong. Emily, who was interested in furthering her education, went first to an Italian convent and later to a French convent to study. Because of her limited English, she was placed in classes with younger girls. She studied piano for a while, but her real interest was in art, especially pencil drawing.

When Emily was seventeen, her mother introduced her to Cecil, her senior by eleven years. He was working with the Douglas line on the *S.S. Haimun*. After only a week, Cecil presented Emily with a beautiful diamond ring. She accepted his gift, not understanding the meaning and his intention to marry her. When Sami explained to her daughter that the ring was a marriage proposal, Emily sent word to Cecil that she intended to go to college and study art. Although she looked up to him and respected him, Emily still retained a strong and independent will. Cecil arrived at Emily's flat feeling he could talk the matter through with her, but she returned the ring. Hurt and angry, Cecil threw the ring to the floor, where it bounced, flew out the window and was lost forever.

Following this exchange, Emily decided to accompany her mother to visit her grandparents and friends in Japan. Cecil, meanwhile, studied for his master's certificate. When Emily returned, the courting continued and Cecil took a serious interest in Emily's desire to continue her education and gave her encouragement. They were wed on April 6, 1910, in Hong Kong.

Marriage to a respectable Englishman would seem to have been the best solution for resolving the question of Emily's future security. But it came with a price. Within three days of the ceremony, Sami Umetsu, for reasons unknown, committed suicide by taking cyanide. She was buried at Happy Valley Cemetery on Hong Kong Island. With no father, no siblings, no homeland, and no mother, Emily's childhood and youth were wiped out by this single act.

As Emily began her life as a married woman, she assumed the dress of a British lady. Photographs of the period show that she was petite, with almond-shaped eyes that underscored her Japanese heritage. She carefully arranged her long, black hair in a wispy chignon at the base of her neck, and she wore exquisite dresses of European design in soft silk fabrics and feminine lace meticulously hand sewn by seamstresses and tailors in Swatow and Hong Kong. Her small stature (she was five feet, four inches tall) spoke to a butterfly-like grace. The lessons of sacrifice, duty and honor, learned so early in her life, had left their imprint, creating an enchanting young woman with the instincts, resilience, and determination of a survivor.

With no immediate families, the young couple found strength in each other. For Cecil, the vast geographical separation and the infrequency of communications had reduced his contact with the Woods of London to occasional and perfunctory correspondence. But in his young wife, however, he discovered a willing and determined student of British civilization. It was not difficult for Emily to embrace her husband's culture, as this helped her to shake off the stigma of being the offspring of two other cultures. Japan had been indifferent toward her in her school years. And the German ancestry had never even been explored: due to the vagaries of different alphabets, neither Emily nor her mother ever knew exactly how to spell Erich von Maline's last name.

. . . .

The city of Alice's birth was a small and quiet place. Swatow—rechristened Shantou (Shan Tou City) by China during the course of the twentieth century—was the antithesis of the energizing bustle that was, and is, Hong Kong. In 1912 it was home to some 15,000 mostly Chinese inhabitants living along the north side of the Han River, which emptied into Swatow harbor. Emily and Cecil Wood were part of a sizeable community of expatriates, most of whom were envoys from trading firms of various European and American origins, including the Scottish Jardine Matheson and Company, the British-American Tobacco Company, and Standard Oil. Swatow had only been opened for foreign trade since 1858 and was initially the center of the opium trade. In the earliest days of the twentieth century, Swatow still was one of old China's seven major commercial centers, but its star was waning.

An inlet from the sea through two narrow entrances formed the harbor that Cecil traveled ceaselessly. The vast open sea lay just beyond. At each entrance to the harbor was a small island: Sugarloaf on the north side, and Masu (also known as Double Island) toward the south. The actual city was about six kilometers from the harbor entrance. Most of the expatriates lived in an area known as the Kialat District. If not by boat, transportation was by rickshaw and sedan chairs, as the roads were narrow, unpaved and entirely unsuitable for automobiles.

The delta that Swatow was located along, at the mouth

of the Han River, had built up over time, so there were few ill-smelling marshes or swamps, which often were part of China's developing landscape. The fresh breath of the South China Sea was ever present, and the rolling hills and surrounding countryside of the Guangdong province fanned out behind. Falling just within the tropical latitudes, Swatow's climate was mild both summer and winter. A strong southwesterly breeze, dubbed the "Swatow doctow," which sprang into existence nearly every afternoon and died out around midnight, mitigated any uncomfortably hot and humid summer days.

In spite of the contrary circumstances attending her birth and the exotic nature of its surroundings, Swatow provided an excellent backdrop and starting point in the long journey of Alice Wood. Her father had established a secure position for himself and was an excellent provider. Her mother was devoted to him, and maintained the British traditions that they both recognized would provide the foundations for the careful upbringing of their children in a foreign land.

Amah's Song

CHAPTER THREE
1912-1918

When time shall have given you memories of the
yester-years I am certain that not least among the gentlefolk whom
you have known you will place Ah Sim, Ah Kah, Yeong Kee and
his boatmen. Therefore should China and the Chinese people
ever be disparaged in your hearing, tell what you yourself know of
them and take pride of rooting for the place where you were born.

Cecil Herbert Wood in a letter to Alice dated June 3, 1939

The Wood children (pictured here on the beach on Masu Island with an
amah) were accompanied by their respective amahs from the moment they
awoke in the morning until they went to bed at night.

Alice went home to Masu, the small island to the south in Swatow's harbor. This first home was well suited to the growing family of Emily and Cecil Wood. Although the birth of a second daughter to a Chinese family would have been a disappointment, Alice was immediately accepted and loved by her parents. She joined sister Edith, her elder by two years, and thirty-two servants in her father's employ, which included boatmen, a cook and helpers, gardeners, upstairs and downstairs maids, houseboys, rickshaw coolies, and nannies, who were called amahs.

As a junior port pilot, Cecil Wood held one of three positions in Swatow that were considered permanent employment. The other two were the senior port pilot and the port doctor. The senior port pilot lived in the city in the Kialat district, and the junior port pilot was based on Masu. The remainder of Swatow's expatriate community was transient, consisting of foreign staff of the customs, post office, missions, and shipping firms who were on rotational assignments and returned to their home countries every two to five years. Even though he was on the payroll of Lloyd's of London, Cecil was essentially self-employed, and could arrange for a "home leave" whenever it suited him. He simply chose not to return to England. Home for the Wood family was Masu, and Masu alone.

Even though the island was later closed to the public—for nearly forty years from the end of World War II until 1979—and has been renamed Mayu, it is still there, bathed in light, salt water and the blended scents of bamboo, banana and jasmine. The black-and-white photos from Alice's early scrapbooks show wild beaches and crashing waves spilling into rocky inlets. The island is completely open to the sea along its eastern edge, where the sun's first rays linger on the shoreline of a sandy beach, one of few in the entire province. Aside from the Wood estate and its separate servants' quarters for the boatmen, there were few major structures, except a striking temple dedicated to the Chinese goddess of the sea, Tianhou, who also was the ancient protector of fisherfolk. The presence of this temple resulted in a cultural oddity: an inordinate number of chickens roamed free, because native Chinese worshippers released them on Masu to honor Tianhou.

As a child, Alice's universe consisted of her family, with its extended members of amahs and servants, and the daily lessons they instilled in her. One of her earliest memories was learning at a missionary school how to sing the Cantonese lyric of the beloved childhood song recorded by Dale Evans, "Jesus Loves Me" and clapping her hands: *"Yes-so oy-ngow ngow gee doe..."* Alice's amah, Ah-Sim, was a fixture in her daily life from the moment she opened her eyes in the morning until she put out the lamp each evening. She was a small but sturdy young woman who wore her black hair lacquered straight back in a long, tightly woven braid down her back and bangs fluttering across her forehead. Alice loved to watch in the mirror of her dressing table as Ah-Sim gently used a silver brush to stroke Alice's long blond curls before bedtime.

As was typical of the period, Ah-Sim was a farm girl from the province. Hailing from a large family, she had no education and little prospect of ever marrying or having a family of her own. Compared to the fate of a less-fortunate group of young girls in the Guangdong province, who were given away very young in marriage (usually to a poor farmer) or sold, she was considered lucky to have obtained employment with a colonial family that had long-term prospects of remaining in China.

Swatow was known less for its agricultural output than for its exquisite needlework. Many girls—often as young as six years old—were sold for a small sum by poverty-stricken parents to local embroidery factory owners. The girls slept on small pallets and their meager possessions included a change of clothing and a rice bowl that would be filled with some rice and a drizzle of vegetables twice a day. Working tediously, their little fingers were trained only to make fine, intricate stitches on linen handkerchiefs, bath and bed linens, and tablecloths. Hunched over their work with eyes squinting inches away from the fabric they sewed ensured a high standard of workmanship. The little girls created seemingly impossible delicate ribbons of windflowers, fans, and petit-point patterns on tea towels and handkerchiefs. This needlework, which dates back 1,000 years before Europe incorporated this skill, was prized by affluent Chinese and colonial Europeans, most of whom were ignorant of the reality that many of these workers often went blind by the age of twenty.

Located just a few miles away from these dimly lit workrooms and factories, the center of town bustled with the activity of distinct "classes." While Chinese peasants crowded the dusty streets with their bamboo cages filled with ducks and chickens, the Chinese of the upper class passed hours in tea houses, sipping fragrant tea and playing the game of mah-jongg.

Ah-Sim had a comfortable but spartan room near the nursery on the second floor at the back of the Woods' spacious wooden home. There, she took complete responsibility for the safety and well being of her young charge. She spoke a Swatow dialect and not a word of English. When she traveled with the family to Hong Kong, the people there could not understand her.

As with most amahs, Ah-Sim's small stature and quiet demeanor belied her strength and vigilance, much the same way that the local wisteria vine's delicate flowers, stirring with the slightest breath of wind, obscure its sinuous branches that cling like iron bands to whatever supports them. When Alice and her sister Edith tired of walking the deep sand of the rough beaches of the island, this tiny amah could hoist at least one and usually both girls onto her back. And while Alice and Edith enjoyed morning tea and fruit with their parents, the amahs waited patiently within earshot, prepared to softly click their tongues with a sound that meant it was time to hurry them off to a more complete English breakfast in the heavily draped and formal dining room.

It was on Masu that Alice developed a primal love of the sea, encouraged by her father, who also had fallen in love with the sea at an early age. Of course, living on an island, with open ocean to the east and an expanse of water to the west, it is not hard to understand why: the sea dominated the Wood family's existence and determined the very rhythm of their life. Alice's earliest recollections were the smells of the sea and feeling the sting of the salt spray as she swam and frolicked with her older sister Edith on the unspoiled beaches.

In the midst of this paradise there were many memories that were not so pleasant, as civil war had broken out among the Chinese. There were violent times with executions for all to see. "One night, my sister Edith and I were trying to sleep when we heard some shots," Alice would later write. "We were in a four-poster bed with mosquito netting all around. We sat up abruptly and, fortunately, went down again just in the nick of time before a bullet whizzed over our heads, tearing the netting. Father and Mother were up on the roof watching the fighting below."

At an early age, Alice rode out to the ships with Cecil, and stayed close to her handsome father as he and his crew of oarsmen escorted ships both into and out of the harbor crowded with steamships and gunboats. The junior port pilot cut a dashing figure standing ramrod straight and looking British to the core. Period photographs consistently depict a man who was meticulous about his appearance, whether clad in his captain's uniform of "plus fours" or in the crisp linen suits that were *de rigueur* in Swatow's subtropical climate.

Among his many letters to Alice, Cecil wrote one to cheer her as she lay recovering from having her appendix removed. It contains a passage illustrating the jolly, playful essence of this self-made man who seemed completely at ease with himself:

One day romping with you and Edith playing horsey I was prancing about with you on my back and Edith wanted me to do the same with her. You were only a little thing but Edith then was quite a lump of a child. However, I thought I was fit enough [from recent surgery] and I didn't like to disappoint her, poor thing. So I took her up on my back and commenced to jump about with her as I had been doing with you. I felt a sharp pain... The muscles had been insufficiently knit to bear Edith's weight and had collapsed under it...So you see, my dear, for one little lapse, just because I didn't want to hurt a child's feelings, I have had to go carefully for 20 years—no tennis or cricket or recreation as other men have—and always in fear of what may happen in those few occasions when I have taken the risk of an easy game of tennis.

Yet Captain Wood spent the bulk of his days escorting ships into and out of Swatow's treacherous harbor (which hid a complex sandbar) as well as inspecting ships, so the children's early education fell to Emily. She was more than up to the task, politely but firmly focusing her children on specific tasks, and never allowing them to be interrupted or distracted by others until the exercise had been successfully completed. Emily encouraged both Edith and Alice to play the piano and to sew. She managed the activities and welfare of the large household staff, keeping the key to the storeroom, which housed all the family supplies. Like a darting hummingbird, Emily seemed to be everywhere at once: supervising the elaborately presented British-style meals prepared by the cook, playing the piano, or poised over her own sewing and embroidery work. In her twilight years, she used brushes and watercolors to recreate tranquil scenes of this idyllic part of her life.

English was spoken at all times in the home. Emily, who spoke English well but naturally with an Asian accent and rhythm mixing up her r's and l's, often despaired that her daughters would speak neither English nor Cantonese properly since some of the amahs spoke in a pidgin blend of both languages. Edith and Alice both attended the local missionary school to ensure proper elocution of English as well as some command of the basics of Cantonese.

The home reserved for the junior port pilot on the island was a two-story wooden colonial construction with a tiled roof and vast verandas on all four sides overlooking courtyard gardens thick with bamboo. It functioned as an island within an island: a complete world revolving around meeting the day-to-day living requirements of the junior port pilot, his wife and their growing family, which also included a small stable of pets—including Tibby, a bull terrier, and Johnson, one of the first in a long line of beloved Siamese cats.

As the primary employer and patriarch to a growing family, Cecil was the unquestioned head of daily life on Masu. He fulfilled this role with discipline, kindness and tact, even when it led to increased responsibilities, as evidenced in this later letter to Alice:

The No. I gigman's [boatman] baby has just died of smallpox. He is very grieved and we are sorry for him. I made him bring all his family to the house and I vaccinated them all myself. Mother and I and everyone in the house, the gigmen, all the cook's family have been vaccinated also. The Alert's engineer wanted to be vaccinated also. He brought his wife and three children so I vaccinated all those five. I am getting quite expert at scratching people's arms. Shall

I do you when you come home?

The two young girls were joined by a younger brother when Alice was about three years old: Eric Thorsby was born February 21, 1915, and was christened in honor of the father that Emily had never known. Aside from the lessons supervised by their mother, all three children enjoyed carefree childhoods in an island setting. Only one major event rocked their early lives, and it did so quite literally. A sharp earthquake struck, shaking their island with a tremendous force. Alice, then about five, recalled that she was with Ah-Sim and her infant brother in the walled garden when it struck. She could hear Edith practicing the piano, then saw her mother run out of the house with her sister just as part of the house collapsed. Ah-Sim guided everyone into a bamboo thicket, where the deep roots ensured safe shelter until the shocks subsided. The family servants promptly built a temporary shelter, and the Wood family (Cecil was on his boat in the harbor when the quake hit, and returned home without incident) camped there in the garden for several weeks until the house had been thoroughly inspected and repaired.

The Woods rarely traveled. There were a number of good reasons for this. First, they lived in a colonial paradise. Second, although Cecil still corresponded with his family in England and maintained a relationship, his homeland was very far away and the method of transportation was by steamship, which was long and arduous. Cecil's older brother, Algernon, remained in London and became a successful jeweler. Algernon's son would eventually leave for Australia and settle there. Cecil's younger brothers, Montagu and Willoughby (who were known to the children only as Uncle Mont and Uncle Willie) had left for Canada and its promise of New-World careers and futures. Willoughby served in the Canadian Army in World War I and died shortly afterward. Cecil's sister, Dorothy, was a very talented pianist and very special to him. She died in London in 1921. For a staunchly British Cecil and his family, South China was now home and they were content with the life they had made for themselves there.

Emily did make one attempt to reconnect with her Japanese roots. When Eric was still a toddler, Emily took all three of her children to meet her aging grandparents, who still lived in the tiny fishing hamlet where she had been raised. It was a difficult and long journey. Once in Japan, Eric contracted diphtheria and would likely have died if not for a doctor who was travelling through by train. He agreed to visit the family and administer the needed medicines. The increasingly aggressive posture of Japan in the 1920s and 1930s barred any future visits.

By the time Alice was five, Cecil had achieved the status of senior port pilot and moved his family into premiere real estate in the Kialat district, where the vast majority of the Swatow expatriate community lived. It had been hard to leave Masu Island, but the house there was permanently intended for the use of the junior port pilot. Besides, the Wood family was growing up, and it was better that children and parents no longer would have to cross an expanse of water to get into town, as the currents were treacherous. Masu was not completely deserted by the Wood family, however. Cecil eventually owned most of the island and the family visited it often for beach outings.

The Woods' Swatow home was large and impressive. Throughout the rooms, elaborately carved furniture made of teak and Foochow flower wood sat atop Tientsin carpets. In one corner of the living room sat Emily's beautiful upright piano, while Chinese and Satsuma vases and ivory elephants and Buddhas added an Asian air to the British surroundings. Emily entertained guests in her formal dining room staffed with servants dressed in black and white uniforms, using Dresden china, two silver tea services, gold finger bowls and jade cups.

Cecil was comfortable in his Kialat home with its spacious twenty-eight rooms, but he was especially at ease surrounded by his collection of instruments and machines, which helped him perform his duties. He loved to show Alice how to work the all-wave radio, and to read the barometers and barograph. Together, they would use his long, polished telescope to look at the constellations and out to the sea that he loved. He diligently ran his business affairs with the help of his two typewriters, a copying press and an adding machine. And during their leisure hours, the family chose from a collection of two hundred records to play on the record cabinet.

With its prescribed order, scores of servants, and all the laughter, tears, and chatter of the growing Wood family, their comfortable colonial life in Swatow seemed far from a fragile existence. Indeed, over the years, the land under it would quake again and the seas would rise up to engulf it, but while nature frequently threatened, it never conquered. It would take the intervention of man—a merciless combination of ruthless bombardment and barbaric invasion by the occupying army of the Japanese Empire—to at last put an end to the idyllic way of life that Alice enjoyed as a child.

A Time for Making Choices

CHAPTER FOUR
1919-1930

I learned at a very tender age how precious life is, and also that though we might like to have complete control of our lives, we never really do. That is why we must have faith in God, and in ourselves to survive.

Alice Wood Bulkeley
Recounting the survival of a typhoon in Swatow

Eric, Alice, and Edith in their pith helmets.

As boarding school was the accepted standard for the education of the children of the British Empire, a shy six-year-old Alice and her older sister were escorted to a prestigious school in Hong Kong, several hundred miles down the South China coast from Swatow. The Diocesan Girls' School (DGS), an institution that has weathered both wars and changing political regimes, still endures today on the Kowloon side of Hong Kong. It still maintains its credo of "Daily Giving Service"—inseparable from the school as it incorporates its initials. At the time, the DGS was the only Protestant school in Southeast Asia where a purely English education could be undertaken. The local Anglican Church had operated the school since its founding in 1860, but it was ruled on a day-to-day basis with the firm hand of a series of headmistresses, including one Miss Sawyer. Photographs of a tight-lipped woman wearing steel-rimmed glasses confirm her as the embodiment of one of those formidable, no-nonsense women who were such stock characters in the novels of Frances Hodgson Burnett and later, in many films starring the young Shirley Temple. Except for Christmas and summer holidays—and one year spent abroad— Alice spent the next decade of her life at the DGS.

The DGS was, in fact, one of the few options available to Cecil and Emily as the parents of "Eurasian" children in the late 1910s and 1920s. The Wood children were considered to be of mixed blood, hence not true Europeans. It did not matter that the family scrupulously observed British custom. In spite of Emily's firm command of English and embrace of British traditions, the family's central role in the expatriate community in Swatow, and Cecil Wood's distinguished lineage, it was not then possible for the children to attend boarding school in England. Secretly, their parents were probably delighted to have to send their children only a relatively short distance away in Hong Kong.

The high brick walls of the DGS and its dormitories filled with spartan iron beds must have stood in sharp contrast to a windswept island and a gracious, friendly, comfortable family home. "Daily Giving Service" quickly became Alice's ritual. Almost immediately upon arrival, her long blond curls were tightly braided and pinned close to her head, since unruly tresses were deemed sinful in an Anglican institution and had to be kept out of sight. Alice cried much of the time during her first weeks, with Edith comforting her as best she could. Amahs became a distant memory, even though older students cared for the youngest DGS pensioners. The older girls, called "school mothers," promptly taught their young charges to take care of themselves, obey rules and traditions, prepare to suffer a tongue lashing or even corporal punishments for minor infractions and, above all, apply themselves to their studies.

Even so, the Wood sisters developed quite a reputation for getting themselves into trouble. In their early years at the DGS, Edith and Alice tended to raise a "bit of a rumpus," according to Alice, especially in their dormitory at night while they were supposed to be saying prayers. Alice also developed into an avid reader, so she often continued her reading well past the lights out at 9 P.M. with the aid of a smuggled flashlight. Whenever she was caught, Alice clasped her hands and pretended to pray in order to avoid punishment. If she was sent for a paddling, she prepared herself by secretly stuffing her bloomers with paper to soften the blows. In later years, the sisters were nearly expelled for regularly speaking to British soldiers on horseback from the school's washroom windows—"a lot of innocent fun," as Alice recalled the incident.

All DGS students worshiped every Sunday at nearby St. Andrew's Church on Nathan Road. They walked two by two in a long line they referred to as "The Crocodile." Alice and Edith, ever interested in activities that took them outside the high walls of their school, volunteered to be in the church choir. They also participated in the Girl Guides, where they met a lovely young girl, Kittie Tse, who would become Alice's lifelong friend. Their outstanding troop was awarded the "Prince of Wales" banner, a coveted honor.

The girls also had other responsibilities, which included caring for and tidying their teachers' bedrooms. Most were single women, although in many cases, this was due to fate, not choice. Alice remembered the poignancy of each November 11 as they retired to their rooms in mourning for fiancés and lovers lost in the carnage of World War I.

Beyond the confines of the DGS, however, lay the splendid port of Hong Kong. The pulsing, frenetic city was a revelation, even if it was politely screened and framed at a distance by the DGS. But it was impossible for Miss Sawyer to shut it out completely. Alice loved to ride the Star Ferry—which remains very much today like it was during her childhood. These "green beetles" as they were called (because of their color and the way they skittered over the water) were each named for a star—the *Morning Star*, the *North Star*—and deftly operated by Chinese sailors in royal blue uniforms. Although the ferries were divided into three classes, British passengers always rode in first class. Alice would take her place there and study the many faces of the people traveling. As she was quite small, she either slipped on board without paying a fare, or, if she was spotted, half-fare. She took it all in: the majestic harbor, sharp hills rising dramatically from the sea, the noisy crowds, the smells and the bustle of people carrying their wares in baskets slung on bamboo poles across their backs, and the wiry rickshaw coolies running barefooted, weaving miraculously through the hordes of people.

If it was a jarring shift from her placid home to the hidebound traditions of a demanding and rigid school, Alice still adapted quickly and excelled in her studies. She made fast friends with other daughters of expatriate parents from a wide range of countries—Britain, of course, but also Canada, India, the United States, France, Denmark, Germany, Japan, and Thailand. Her school progress reports were uniformly excellent, and she received regular letters from her parents full of encouragement and praise. Cecil and Emily also regularly sent the girls care packages and crates of fresh fruit to supplement the bland school diet.

Cecil, in particular, guided his younger daughter through his insights into the ultimate rewards of an educa-

Hilda Alice Wood, ca. 1914.
Born in 1912 to a Japanese/German mother and an
English father, she was raised British—a true child of
the twentieth century.

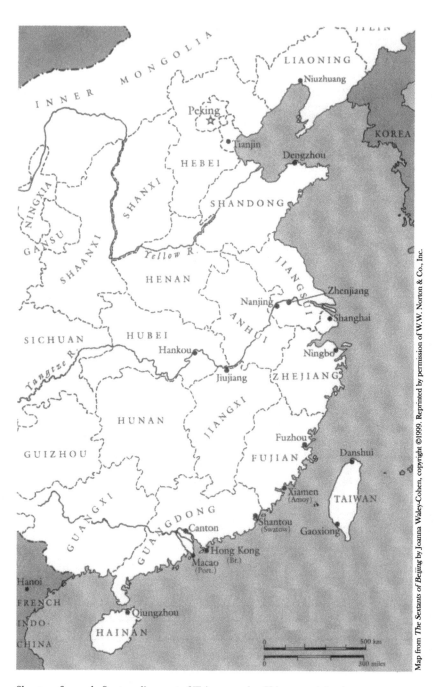

Shantou, formerly Swatow, lies west of Taiwan on the Chinese mainland.

A view across Swatow harbor, 1920s. Although never a serious rival to either Shanghai or Hong Kong, Swatow briefly ranked as the third busiest port in China in the early 1930s. This afforded a comfortable living for its senior port pilot, Cecil Wood.

In the late 1910s, Emily Wood made one pilgrimage to Japan to introduce her children (left to right) Edith, Alice and Eric, to the grandparents who had raised her near Nagasaki. The family's suitcases can be seen at far left.

Clockwise from top: A demanding motto, derived from the Diocesan Girls' School's initials; Alice and Edith in their 1918 DGS winter uniforms and hairstyles; A period sketch of the DGS main building, Kowloon.

Alice (balancing left) eagerly sought out all activities, including ballet, that let her escape the strict confining regimine of the DGS.

Cecil Wood, senior port pilot, was an anchor of the British expatriate community of Swatow.

Emily Wood, flanked by Edith and Alice, on the beach at Masu Island, 1920. The girls sport the summer uniforms of the Diocesan Girls' School.

The Wood family residence at 73 Kialat Road, Swatow. Wide verandas overlooked courtyards, a tennis court and Emily's garden, thick with bamboo and scented by jasmine.

A rare interior shot of the colonial décor and furnishings of the Wood home in Swatow includes Emily's beloved upright piano—the instrument that was seen floating across the living room during a deadly typhoon.

Eric and Alice enjoy a moment of lookalike tomfoolery.

Although the Wood family left their home on Masu Island for Swatow when Alice was very young, the beaches on Masu remained a popular escape for weekend swims and walks.

A doubles tennis tournament in the Wood garden in 1920s Swatow. Playing tennis was a year-round possibility in the subtropical climate. Alice and Edith can be seen in the foreground, wearing their school uniforms.

During her university years, Alice (seated, second from right) excelled at track and field competitions, earning numerous medals and setting records in the 100-yard dash.

Alice Wood was among the first women graduates of the University of Hong Kong in 1934.

Alice (third from right) and the "Gay Nineties Girls" danced the can-can at the Hong Kong Peninsula Hotel's South Pacific Ball in April 1939 to raise money for war-torn China.

One of the last photos of the Woods before World War II, gathered here in Hong Kong to celebrate the christening of Edith's son, Richard (in Edith's arms). Her daughter, May, is at her side. Emily is second from left, with Edith's husband, Arthur, in front of her. Emily's youngest daughter, Leilah, stands closest to the camera. Alice is second from right. At far left is Miss Sawyer, the DGS headmistress.

tion. His letters to Alice must have had a completely different tone from those that Edith—a less-enthusiastic student—received. Alice and Edith remained inseparable in spite of being polar opposites in almost every way. Edith bore a strong resemblance to her mother's Japanese forebears, with straight black hair and twinkling brown eyes. Alice was the counterpoint: petite, with blue eyes and blond wavy hair that favored her father's English bloodline. Gone, however, were the girlish curls, as both girls now wore their hair in a fashionably short tomboyish style. Years later, Edith would expand on their differences:

> *As time went by we both grew older and Alice became quite a brain and did very well in all the school exams. Came to the top of her class, whereas I was not so clever. That caused me to envy her. Alice was very good in track and field events right through to the University and became quite an athlete winning many trophies. As we grew older, we became closer and now I have a deep affection for my sister and love her dearly.*

The decade spent at the DGS settled into a regular pattern: dedicated family correspondence, birthday parcels, peaceful visits home in the summertime and joyous Christmas holidays celebrated with formal parties, traditional Christmas crackers, plum pudding and presents. Being that the official British school year began in January and concluded in November, the girls experienced the challenges of living with other girls at various ages and stages of development. In addition to her parents, Alice maintained an extensive correspondence with Eric, her witty and precocious brother. On their return trips to

Swatow, which involved an overnight steamship trip supervised by a captain who was invariably a friend and colleague of Cecil's, classmates often accompanied the Wood children to enjoy the vacation atmosphere of Swatow and the Wood family's generous hospitality in their spacious and friendly home.

The circumstances of her Eurasian status later surfaced in school, and became clear to Alice during her middle-school years. One day, sitting in class, wearing the prescribed navy blue jumper (for winter) or white (for summer) uniform, she was asked to complete a form, along with all the other girls in the class. One line of the form requested nationality and Alice wrote in "English." The teacher, observing her pupils as she walked up and down the rows of desks, observed what Alice had just written. She told Alice, "You are not English, but Eurasian." The remark stayed with Alice—who later recalled it in an interview regarding her youth—striking her primarily as an illogical statement.

To me there was no such country as Eurasia. I was a British subject. At that age I was pretty cocky, and doing well in school. It came as a shock to me, and I knew I was going to face some difficulties. Instead of thinking less of myself I was even more determined to be proud of my mixed blood.

This determination eventually manifested itself as pride —another sinful quality. Once, when Alice was sent to Miss Sawyer's office, she found herself being scolded for behaving like a "poppy cock," a British colloquialism for a snob. The dour headmistress also took issue with Alice's "high and mighty ways." Cecil, immediately upon hearing of the incident, wrote his daughter a thoughtful letter that included this passage:

> *...When you are being scolded, don't put on an aggrieved or sulky look that only makes teachers angry. Just listen politely and attentively to what is being said to you, whether you deserve it or not, for you are having an extra lesson for free....Educated gentlefolk do not hesitate to express sorrow, even if they themselves have done no harm nor caused any annoyance, whenever a possibility of having done so occurs.*

When Alice was eight, the potent combination of nature's wrath and the ever-uncertain political situation in China forced Cecil and Emily to re-evaluate the choices they had made for their children so they could make better decisions for their children's future.

Late one day in the summer of 1920 during summer holiday in Swatow, Alice noticed that the sky had changed to frightening colors. The sunset was like no other she had ever seen: with night approaching, the sinking sun was an intense orange, with vivid black and yellow patches of light filtering from threatening clouds. That particular day had been no different than any other summer day—hot and humid as was the custom in summer, except it was unusually still. The daily cooling breeze, nicknamed the "Swatow doctow," had not stirred that afternoon.

The doctow made summers more tolerable to the expatriate European community in those years without air conditioning, and was something of a faithful friend as it swept gently across the harbor every afternoon, rustling bamboo and spreading the cool scent of jasmine. It allowed the Wood family and others to enjoy the shade of their wide verandas or a quick match of tennis, instead of retreating behind brick walls in search of a darker, cooler place where they could fan themselves.

The sky that evening portended one of the most violent typhoons in the history of the South China Sea. Alice went to bed early that evening, only to be awakened by her amah when the storm struck. Picking up mattresses as they fled the room, the amahs and other house servants ushered Edith, Alice, Eric and Edith's visiting friend, Ellen, downstairs into the living room—the most central portion of the house. Cecil and Emily met them there after working with the remaining servants to close all the shutters and seal off outer rooms. The rising moan of the wind and rain as the eye of the storm approached and the deafening sound of trees crashing into buildings kept the group awake. The children were more excited than frightened.

As the wind died back, Alice went back to sleep thinking that the storm was over. It was during the calm that they began to notice a more ominous sound—that of rising water. It streamed in under doors, through the walls, and rose up through the cracks in the floorboards. The water continued to rise, even as the wind began howling again outside. When it reached to Cecil's knees, he hoisted Edith to his shoulders and walked resolutely to the front door. It was in vain that he tried to open it. The force of the water rushing against it outside made him abandon the idea of leaving the house in a mad dash to find higher ground. The children noticed a stream of black rising from the water and spreading in lines up the living room walls, realizing in amazement that these were actually beetles and cockroaches in desperate pursuit of higher ground, too!

The relentless rise finally sparked terror in both Cecil's and Emily's eyes. The family retreated up the staircase, the water following them up each step. "Please God, help us!" Cecil cried, cursing the day he ever set foot in China. The last sight that greeted their eyes from downstairs was the piano floating on its side across the living room.

As the water reached fourteen feet inside the house, the Wood family abandoned the staircase and crowded into a large second-floor bathroom. Cecil and Emily installed the children, wrapped tightly in blankets, in the steel bathtub. The children were finally frightened, especially since both Tibby (who was pregnant) and Johnson were missing. The overnight vigil continued and, gradually, the water slowed, then stopped. The house had held, but most of the heavy tile roof had been blown away and several waterlogged walls were in danger of collapse.

Not one of the Woods' family of servants perished in the typhoon, but more conservative estimates of the time state that at least 60,000 people had drowned. Even Tibby's puppies, which had arrived during the night, were casualties. The poor dog could be seen trying unsuccessfully to pull her drowned litter from the water. Johnson, the Siamese cat, would go missing for two weeks, after which he returned undaunted by his experiences.

From their veranda, the Wood children witnessed swarms of desperate people and a seemingly endless parade of corpses being carted away through the muddy streets. Many were buried in mass graves due to the lack of coffins. Swatow's harbor was a sodden ruin, ships smashed in the harbor and buildings intertwined in a mass of destruction. As the adults cleaned up, the children watched Emily, with her small Mauser, and Cecil, carrying a German Luger, take aim at the rats who scurried around the house.

In 1923, Cecil took an extended leave of absence and removed his three children from their boarding schools (Eric attended the Diocesan Boys School.) Perhaps it was the typhoon experience a few years earlier that influenced his decision. Steamer trunks were packed and they sailed to Canada, where Cecil had investments in land, for a reunion with Cecil's brothers' families who lived in Ontario and Saskatchewan.

In that year, the bulk of the Canadian branch of the Wood clan was the growing family of Cecil's younger brother, Montagu. The brothers and their families, along with Cecil's father, who had come from England, reunited in rural Saskatchewan, where Mont homesteaded a vast acreage received in part as a land grant from the Canadian government. Unfortunately, Alice would not meet her namesake, Cecil's mother, as she had passed away earlier in the year.

United for the first time, Edith, Alice and Eric bonded instantly with their Canadian cousins in the rustic farm setting, enjoying running through pastures and feeding the livestock. Emily, however, did not like the brown-colored drinking water or the fact that they had to go into town for a bath. The South China cousins found it a novelty and quickly adjusted to the cold climate. But, Cecil and Emily, who had come with the secret hope of finding a safer haven with better schools in which to educate their children, were sadly disappointed. A one-room schoolhouse represented all the opportunity that there was in sparsely populated Resource, Saskatchewan. Two sisters ran the Jones School, where they instructed seventy-two children at all levels of primary and secondary education, and it was located four miles away, across cow pastures, from Uncle Mont's appropriately named "Reunion Farms." Cecil and Emily bought schoolbooks for all the children and donated a library for the school.

After several months, Cecil and Emily retreated with their children to the Toronto area, where they attended the more prestigious Fern School for a time. Even though Toronto represented a vast improvement over Resource, Cecil and Emily finally abandoned their original intent: to leave the children behind in boarding schools in the New World while they continued to live and work in Swatow.

So, after the decision was finally made and the travel arrangements in order, the Wood family returned home to Swatow. However difficult and precarious their colonial lifestyle, the family would remain together. They had crossed an ocean only to discover that their true home was the distant shore they had left behind. And on December 28, 1928, that home once more welcomed a new member of the Wood family, Leilah Lois. The family considered her birth a blessing. Emily now had a baby at home and Ah-Sim to care for her.

Re-enrolled at the DGS, Alice plowed headlong into her studies, continuing to heed her father's long-distance counsel. During her final year at the DGS, her dedication bore its fruit: she was appointed Head Girl, a role-model position that she took very seriously. Alice then sat for the DGS final exams, which came from Cambridge in England and were taken at the University of Hong Kong. She graduated as valedictorian of her class.

While life continued at a leisurely pace for Alice, political storm clouds gathered over the Chinese mainland in 1930, the year of her emancipation from the DGS. Japan began executing a number of military maneuvers that would ultimately lead to full-scale invasion, occupation, and war.

Miss Alice Wood in the "Putting the Shot" event for ladies.—(King's Studio).

First Breath of Freedom

CHAPTER FIVE
1930-1934

Alice in wonderland am I
Round all the world I roam
From magic casements for I fly
As bright as fairy foam
I am the dream of all mankind.
The glow of the hearthside fire,
Unattainable, fleet as the wind
I am the world's desire.

Composed by Henry Green, Swatow, South China
(From Alice's diary)

Early on a September day in 1930, the Star Ferry carried a slim young woman across the wind-whipped harbor from Kowloon to Hong Kong Island. With her light-brown, shoulder length hair, angular features, and clad in a simple dress, Alice Wood was a portrait of youthful elegance. For the first time in more than a decade, the ferry crossing would not be a mere day trip, for Alice had at last escaped the iron grip of the Diocesan Girls School: no more uniforms, rigidly prescribed behavior, or Miss Sawyers.

Crossing the harbor with its spectacular setting of rising peaks, crowded with junks and the boat people on their sampans, she was en route to a new life—this time as one of the first female students at Hong Kong University. As was her custom, she stood firmly and breathed in deeply, savoring the salt spray just as she had in her childhood. Except for the directives given in letters sent by both her parents, Alice was at last able to make her own choices.

Her acceptance at the university had been made to seem something of a miracle by her father, who was merely exuberant over the fact that Alice had passed the entrance exams and been accepted on her first attempt. Cecil had written:

Wonderful news this morning. The 13th is your lucky day. The Registrar of the University tells us you have qualified for matriculation and may join the University without further examination.

God bless you, sweetheart, study hard, for the more honors you get the higher our hearts beat for you and the higher we can hold our heads.

I have asked for you to be entered as a member of the University and for Miss Sawyer to arrange for your board, lodging, and tuition.

Like the Diocesan Girls' School, Hong Kong University still operates today, with students attending classes on the steeply sloping campus in some of the original buildings, like the Old Main building, which dates back to the institution's founding in 1910. The main point of difference between the university and her boarding school, then as now, is that Alice's classmates were now mostly young men rather than women. Her easy charm, striking looks, and quick wit soon won her friends as well as admirers.

For the first time in her life, Alice enjoyed an opportunity to live on her own and set some of her own rules. She traded the DGS dormitory with its twelve single beds to a large room and communal bathroom for an apartment with a roommate located near the university, with the luxury of separate bedrooms and bathrooms for each young lady.

While she remained close with her childhood friend, Kittie Tse, the majority of her new friends were young men. Time has reduced them to a roll call of mostly first names: Donald, Reggie, Archie, Ernie, Duggie, Tinker, Mac, Bill, and Granville. Over time, several of these graduated to the status of beaux and even suitors. Alice, however, was enjoying her new-found freedom; she had been a practical-minded girl, so it made little sense to her to get so serious with marriage proposals. She was only in her late teens and quite determined to get an undergraduate degree and continue on to law school. Of course, there were many sporting events—tennis matches, swimming parties, boating regattas—as well as opportunities for stolen kisses and overheated promises. She was able to keep most of the proposals at arm's length, and most of the young men remained her friends.

Donald Anderson certainly ranked highest in the friendship category. Even though he carried a torch for "Allie" (as he called her) throughout his life, he kept up a stream of consistent correspondence with her that included several years spent in England on post-graduate studies to become a barrister.

The political situation in China, already tense, continued to worsen throughout Allie's first year at the university. In the wake of a plotted bombing carried out by Japanese operatives, Japan's aggressive military had seized the capital of Manchuria and then quickly fanned across the rest of the province, beginning one of the twentieth century's most brutal military occupations. China's leaders mistakenly thought that by yielding Manchuria, they could contain the Japanese Imperial expansion with its proclamations of freeing China from evil foreign influences. They could not. With its status as a British crown colony conferring it a measure of protection, Hong Kong—far to the south of Manchuria—was considered to be out of harm's way. Life continued there at its usual pace, and that pace was swift compared to the rest of China.

Alice lived for a time at St. Stephen's Hall at the university, and later moved into a two-bedroom apartment with another female student. This was the first time in her life that she had lived independently. Yet she was far from being lonely. For starters, the Wood family was now well represented in Hong Kong. Her brother and sister both lived in the immediate vicinity. Eric was a pensioner at the Diocesan Boys' School and Edith continued on at the DGS even after Alice left for the university. Edith remained the focus of her parents' worries, particularly when she became enamored of a young man who fell short of Cecil's and Emily's expectations. In a 1933 letter to Alice, Emily confided:

We are still awaiting what has happened between Mr. Hamson and Edith. Father wrote to him a week ago, stating strongly that neither of us consents to their engagement—"No, for all time"—so I do not know what Edith is going to do. I have written to Edith begging her to consider us and not to get engaged or think of getting married yet....

Edith was headstrong and determined that she and Arthur were meant for each other. At first she abided by her parents' orders not to see him. But soon she rebelled against them, continuing their relationship until, unexpectedly, she heard that Cecil had contracted typhoid fever and was gravely ill. Leaving Arthur in Hong Kong, Edith took the ferry to be by her father's side. The family and Cecil's doctor questioned whether he would survive. Cecil did recover and Edith attempted to make peace with him, but didn't request his blessing. She left without it.

Although this family disagreement caused some upheaval, Edith, who was very much in love, remained true to Arthur and married him on September 16, 1933, at St. John's Cathedral in Hong Kong, instead of St. Andrew's Church where they had met. She and Alice, who served as her maid of honor, wore flowing pink gowns embroidered with blue forget-me-nots and matching pink broad-brimmed hats. Miss Sawyer, the girls' former headmistress from the DGS, gave Edith away. It proved to be a good match and they were to enjoy many happy years together. After making their home in Hong Kong, they welcomed a daughter on October 3, 1936. Although Edith had heard little from her father, upon the baby's arrival the new grandparents sent the new parents gifts and a telegram of congratulations with a request—that the child be named Mavis. To keep the peace, they obliged, but came to call their daughter "May" for short. Two years later Edith gave birth to a son, Richard.

Alice meanwhile remained focused on her college courses. At HKU, the competitive spirit from her DGS days was put to good use: she excelled in sports, starring as a sprinter in the one-hundred meter dash. She earned numerous silver cups and many track medals for her victories. Alice continued to do well in her studies, advancing in her coursework almost without incident until her senior year. Leilah boasted about her sister, "She was brilliant, talented and a superb athlete. I have always looked up to her and admired her."

In that last year she experienced another harsh encounter with discrimination—not for being a Eurasian, this time, but on account of her gender. She recalled that her professor for commercial law, a required course for graduation, did not approve of young women attending his class, and Alice was the only one. After final exams, she was stunned to learn that he had failed her and only her. In those years, failing one class resulted in the student repeating the entire academic year.

Both the pace and structure of the curriculum had to be challenging to a young woman outnumbered ten-to-one by competitive undergraduate men. But thanks to her firm foundation from the DGS and the support of her father, Alice met each challenge with dedication, politeness, and consistency. And at the end of 1934—after five years—Alice was awarded her undergraduate degree.

Love and War

CHAPTER SIX
1934-1939

And still shall recollections trace
In fancy's mirror ever near,
Each smile, each tear—that familiar face;
Though lost to sight, to memory dear.

The first entry in Alice's diary of 1937.

Alice and John in a moment of fun during their courtship.

.

In June 1934, with her college degree in hand, Alice returned to Swatow seeking employment. Cecil had heard of a secretarial job at Butterfield & Swire, a British shipping company, and inquired for Alice after she had completed a qualifying course. She was accepted and went to work as a confidential secretary for Gordon Campbell, the firm's manager.

By 1936 her childhood home had become an eerily quiet place. Emily and Leilah had been evacuated to Hong Kong with the rest of the British women and children, away from the hostilities in Swatow. Edith and her family already lived in Hong Kong and Eric was now in his last year at the University of Hong Kong. Swatow itself, however, was far from quiet. Aerial bombing by the Japanese was a common occurrence and Chinese men, women, and children were often brutalized, shot, hanged, or beheaded in the streets. Japanese planes flew in low around the district, taunting and terrorizing citizens, and air raid sirens became a common interruption. Many roofs, including that of the Wood house, had been painted with an enormous British flag, as a signal to the Japanese not to inadvertently bomb these buildings. British and American buildings were off-limits at this point—before those countries had officially entered the war.

Alice took her job very seriously and got along well with Campbell and his wife Mary. He knew that she could be counted on under any circumstances and he came to rely on her excellent work. Because members of the office worked with the constant uncertainty of their safety in Swatow, they were brought even closer together personally by the daily risks they shared.

Although her secretarial career was set against the backdrop of a war zone, Alice's social life was amazingly lively. After work, she met with friends for tennis at her home or met at the International Club for dinner, dances, and movies. Many of her friends from the University remained in her life, including Donald, Tinker, Bill, and Kittie. In her nightly diary entries, Alice kept track of the letters she wrote to each friend and of the letters she received in return. Many from the men talked of marriage proposals. In Alice's mind, she had always imagined she would end up the wife of a nice British chap, so these proposals seemed to follow in her general life plan. The world around her may have been falling apart, but she continued on her chosen course as any woman in her twenties would, oblivious that her world was becoming increasingly dangerous and unsure.

To the men in her circle, Alice was a vivacious, intelligent presence, and they continued to vie for her hand in marriage. By 1936 Donald had returned to London to study law and prepare for the bar examinations, but his love for Alice never quite ended. He wrote to remind her that he remembered her girlish giggle and inviting smile. He also warned "Allie" about Tinker, who had asked her to marry him. Donald felt Tinker lacked a certain honor and courage. Alice continued to see all her friends socially, but became increasingly close to Bill, who possessed an especially sensitive view of the world and love, perhaps overly sensitive in such a time of war and upheaval.

. . . .

On the evening of October 12, 1937, a Tuesday night, Alice and Cecil accepted a dinner invitation aboard the HMS *Diana*, a British warship anchored in Swatow harbor. The ship's officers had invited a few British civilians aboard for a farewell dinner from 6 to 8 P.M., along with the officers of the *Sacramento*, a U.S. Navy coastal gunboat in the shared harbor that had been evacuating American women and children from China. The *Sacramento*, or *"Sacchy,"* was affectionately referred to by her crew as "the Galloping Ghost of the China Coast." It was the last ship of the U.S. Navy with a white hull, steam engines, and sails resembling a large yacht.

Following Cecil up the ship's ladder, she courteously shook hands with the impressive row of smart-looking uniformed officers. Naturally they were delighted to meet such an attractive woman, and she welcomed a chance to be part of "another world" for an evening. One young American ensign dressed in a pointed "fore-and-aft" hat and heavily adorned with gold shoulder boards—John Duncan Bulkeley—spotted her immediately as she made her way up the line. Seeing her mischievous eyes and dazzling smile, he was enamored from their first words. In that one moment, their destinies became irrevocably bound.

Throughout the evening John managed to occupy Alice's time. They chatted about Swatow and themselves.

John had graduated from the U.S. Naval Academy in 1933, shaking the hand of President Roosevelt as he accepted his hard-earned diploma. John was eager to go to sea and echoed the famous quote by John Paul Jones, who was buried beneath the Naval Academy chapel: "Give me a fast ship, for I intend to go in harm's way." From his time in the Boy Scouts, and later as an Eagle Scout, he never had second thoughts about serving his nation and its Constitution, and answering this calling; they were his bedrock, and the spread of democracy and equality his purpose. John would not be commissioned in the navy until the following year. Half of his graduating class had to wait due to the Congressional budget. He took a one-year Depression leave before being commissioned in the navy and shipping out on the cruiser *Indianapolis*. Alice's accomplishments at Hong Kong University must have impressed him, although she was modest and not one to boast.

Alice asked John if he played tennis and suggested he come by her home sometime to play a few sets with her friends. By the time Alice got to her diary that night, young Bulkeley rated a brief entry: "Met young American Officer. J.B. Club till 9 p.m." She would later record the following about their courtship:

> *On our first meeting, I saw a rather boyish looking young man with a zest for life and terrific drive, with the navy blue and gold running through his veins. We talked for hours on our first dates, and I felt he was draining me of all my thoughts and experiences. His courage and strength were very evident to me, and I felt that if ever I was in trouble he would come*

*through for me, or for that matter anyone who called
upon him for help. And beneath that rough exterior
I came to see a sensitive and compassionate man,
one who had been hurt deeply, and one who did not
intend to be hurt again. This made for the complex-
ity of the man I came to know, admire and love.*

Before a week had lapsed from their first meeting,
John had taken Alice up on the tennis invitation. They
played one set and went out that evening, dancing until 1
A.M. The following night included dinner and a movie on
the *Sacramento* and Alice wrote, "Lovely night. John—
nice boy." Thursday, Friday, and Saturday of the same
week included tennis again and more dinner and dancing. Meanwhile, all other suitors were put temporarily on
hold, including Bill.

On Sunday, John called at 6 P.M. and Alice and Leilah
went for dinner on the *Sacramento*. Since Leilah spoke
the Swatow dialect and Alice didn't, the couple often took
her along on their dates to act as their interpreter. But by
9 P.M. that night, Leilah was feeling unwell and asked to
go home. John insisted on walking the two girls home.
Once Leilah was safe inside, Alice took John up to her
retreat on the roof of the house, which could only be ac-
cessed through a tricky series of steps up from one of the
verandas. Leilah knew where they went but said nothing.
They talked for what seemed like hours as they looked
out onto the silhouettes of trees and rooftops and the flick-
ering lights of Swatow, while John watched for signals from
his ship. The calmness of the night was punctuated at times
by the crack of gunfire, but the two were deep in conversation about life and what they each hoped from it.

Alice was surprised by John's openness and sensitivity, and especially his certainty of his future. Her group of boys suddenly seemed like just that—boys. Their proposals now seemed hollow. Each one was less sure than the other of his future in the atmosphere of war in China. John was certain of his role in this war and felt positive about its outcome. He wasn't quite brash, but he was confident. And he was sure that he wanted Alice in his future. To him, she was much more than any American girl he had met at home. Alice was refined, the product of a proper British family and a boarding school education. She had her own air of confidence and had accomplished things other girls didn't dare at the time—graduating from the university, setting athletic records, and living in a war zone that practically every other woman had fled in terror months ago.

That night, any questions Alice had about John were forgotten in a kiss so powerful that she was swept off her feet. They found in that instant that they were intellectually and magically connected. She felt a wave of strength in his embrace and felt secure. Alice had had many boyfriends, but she had never experienced a man like this. Here was an American from the other side of the world and she still had Donald, Tinker, and Bill committing their love for her. But John had captured her heart.

The roof became their favorite retreat from the crazy turbulence of Swatow below. From there, the *Sacramento* could signal John using lights to get him back on board in a hurry. Alice would listen intently to his amazing stories of life in America and in the navy. She found herself falling for this dashing and courteous man with his calling to serve his country. By the following Tuesday, October 26,

Alice's diary read: "John wants to marry me in a year's time." And by Saturday, "Realise J is the one and only."

On November 2, at 2 P.M., Alice watched as the *Sacramento*—with John on board—left for Hong Kong. Suddenly she felt a bit shaken out of his spell. Were the past two weeks just a foolish affair? Maybe he wouldn't write as he had promised. A week went by without a single letter.

During that week, Bill came back into the picture. With John gone, Alice picked up her usual social whirl of friends, and Bill was there for dinner and dancing at the club. Alice told herself that maybe she should be sensible and focus on Bill. He was wonderful and matched her in conversation and wit. When they were together, John seemed a distant memory. Until John's first letter arrived, and then another. He sent magazines and letters and talked about the plans they had discussed on the roof. Alice decided it might be better not to see Bill quite so often, for he clouded her judgment.

Alice decided to talk to Lola, a close friend and confidante, about the whole mess. She felt terrible about Bill and still somewhat unsure about John. She felt she had to tell each one about the other. After explaining things to Bill, Alice decided to take a day trip to Masu Island, to walk on the beach and think things through. Bill had originally planned to go with her, but canceled at the last minute, upset with the turn of events in their relationship. That night at the club Bill showed up and caused quite a scene in front of her friends. Poor Bill felt betrayed and couldn't understand how things had changed so quickly. Alice, in fact, was just as surprised herself at how in a matter of days, her entire life had been changed by one man.

But was she making a terrible mistake with Bill? The next morning he rushed over to apologize for his outburst and to offer Alice a plan. They should get married immediately and sail for England. He wrote her lengthy letters begging her not to marry John. She confessed to her diary, "Almost gave in to Bill." But first she needed to see John—immediately. A few short days later, she packed a small bag and boarded the *Anshun* for Hong Kong.

Although it was wonderful to see him again and she was reassured somewhat, doubts about John began creeping into her thoughts. He seemed different. They spent time together when he wasn't on duty and she spent time visiting her mother, sister, and friends around Hong Kong. After a week, she decided to return to Swatow. Maybe he wasn't everything she had imagined up on the roof. She was more confused than ever.

.   .   .   .

For the time being, Alice would try to return to a normal life, which meant Butterfield & Swire during the work week and John when he was in port. When the *Sacramento* was moored in Swatow Harbor, John arranged for a small boat to stand by in the water near her office or at her home in case she wanted to come on board. He constantly worried about her safety, but she never took him up on this offer. John had reason to worry. He had seen the reports about the Japanese Imperial Army.

Between 1937 and 1938, Japanese troops in Nanking killed nearly 370,000 Chinese men, women, and children. Their brutality was gruesome. Men were beheaded, disemboweled and set afire. Women and young girls were savagely raped and often slaughtered afterward. But this

"Rape of Nanking," as it would be called, was just a grim foreword for the estimated 30 million Chinese who would eventually die at the hands of the Japanese.

One afternoon, as the workday came to an end, she could have used a little protection. As she and her fellow employees prepared to leave the office, Japanese planes suddenly began to fly aggressively close overhead. They bombed various strategic targets nearby and the Chinese headquarters not far from Alice's home. As the Butterfield and Swire employees looked around the dock, they noticed Campbell's motor launch, which was always on site to take him to his home on the opposite side of the harbor. As they stood there, they counted nine planes coming toward them and the other employees turned to Alice to ask if they should make a run for it. Confident of her sprinting skills, Alice shouted, "Let's go!" Running for their lives, the group headed for the boat, which took off and headed directly to the safety of the *Sacchy*. But one of the planes spotted them before they reached safety and swooped down, spraying machine-gun fire across the boat. Everyone in the boat flattened out, praying for survival. Miraculously, all escaped unharmed.

John witnessed the aggressive Japanese actions at sea as well. On December 12, 1937, the Japanese sank the American gunboat *Panay* while it patrolled the Yangtze River, not far from the *Sacramento*. John was shown photographs of the bodies of the American sailors, many of whom helplessly floundered in the water, riddled with machine-gun fire. After an apology from the Japanese government, President Roosevelt dropped the matter. But John did not forget the incident, which the sailors knew was a deliberate act of war. He had seen the massive cruelty of the Japanese and his hatred only intensified.

As John and Alice continued to see each other, he became even more aware that her life was in danger. He spent time with Cecil at the Wood home and met with Emily several times when she was home. The Woods were just as fond of John as he was of Alice. Cecil could get lost in conversation about the sea as John recounted tales of his Caribbean travels aboard a Colombian freighter when he was only twelve. Cecil knew John could be Alice's way out of this tumultuous situation, which was deteriorating quickly. Women were being routinely attacked and often raped in the streets by wandering Japanese soldiers who often showed little mercy, even to pregnant women, who they were known to bayonet for sport. After one raid, Alice even lost her private rickshaw driver, a bare-footed, weather-beaten man who "flew" with his rickshaw charge. They had been taking the back roads to avoid the main one, which had been bombed. He became petrified and fled, leaving Alice to commute to work on her bicycle.

At work one day, a bomb of another sort was dropped on Alice. While going through some files at the office, she came across a letter written by Campbell. In it he informed his boss that he intended to keep Alice as his secretary even though the company had a strict policy not to hire Eurasians. All employees were to be purely English or Chinese. This issue once again had slapped her in the face. And now, when she was thinking about marrying an American.

None of this seemed to matter to John. He was certain of his love for Alice, which only grew stronger as they spent more time together during his time in port. Ironically, many of their "dates" were spent on bicycles, touring the bombed areas of Swatow and photographing the unspeakable atrocities committed by the Japanese. The streets were littered with the mutilated corpses of Chinese civilians—including children—who had been caught in the Japanese bombings or shot in the streets as examples of what the soldiers would do to anyone who displeased them. One particular afternoon they witnessed a Chinese man being "crucified" by Japanese soldiers on their bayonets. On another occasion they had to make a mad dash on their bicycles when a group of soldiers noticed Alice and liked what they saw.

.   .   .   .

As the months together continued, Alice's initial remark in her diary about marriage within a year slowly became a reality. She and John became engaged after he proposed to her at the Astor House Hotel in Swatow, the very place of her birth. The couple dined on tomato soup, boiled fish with butter sauce and steamed custard and began to plan for a wedding at St. Andrew's Church in Hong Kong, where Alice had spent so many of her childhood Sundays. She chose her wedding dress and veil and asked Campbell's permission to leave her position with the firm. Knowing that Swatow left little hope for Alice, he gladly wished her well and wrote a glowing recommendation in case she intended to find work with another firm in the future.

Alice waited to schedule the ceremony to coincide with the *Sacramento's* schedule and planned on port visits. This became increasingly frustrating. John kept in constant contact as best as he was able to by telegram. On October 16, 1938, he cabled from Shanghai: "Intend to consummate plans first November if convenient to you Shanghai or Hong Kong depending on situation. Can you be ready? Love, John."

Alice hurriedly packed and said a tearful good-bye to her father. She sent a return cable to John and took the first B & S ship to Shanghai. This sprawling city of more than 7 million had undergone many changes itself in the past year and was now the second largest city in the world. Prior to 1937, it was a city of contrasts, with the European section busy with banks and flourishing businesses. The darker side of the city hid opium dens, bars, and brothels. Through all this bustle, Chinese men and women would rickshaw, pedicab, or run with their swaying bamboo yokes loaded down with their wares through jostling crowds of people. But as the Japanese took over, "liberating the Chinese from the Europeans," they set up checkpoints and enforced rationing. Parts of the city sometimes went without electricity and water. Food became scarce.

Alice arrived with her wedding dress and veil and all the necessary papers, uncertain of the outcome. John was there to meet her upon her arrival. They went immediately to the Metropole Hotel, where he had reserved a room with twin beds for "Lieutenant (j.g.) (junior grade) Bulkeley and wife." As she entered the room, Alice was overcome by the scent of several bouquets of yellow roses. She was deeply touched by his gesture. But now they had to turn their attention to the business at hand—a wedding without a single family member present.

Captain Allen, the skipper of the *Sacramento,* had offered to give Alice away, but suddenly the couple found a mass of red tape to overcome before they could tie the knot. John's ship was moored on the Whangpoo River, quite a long way from their hotel, and he was on duty almost every other day. On November 10, Alice received a cable from her father. He told her that if she and John hadn't been married by then, he wanted her to come home immediately. Although Cecil liked John, he was worried that Alice would become one more woman enjoyed by a sailor and left alone in a hotel room with promises of married life.

When John came into Shanghai early that day, Alice showed him the cable and they set out in earnest to be married immediately. They dashed over to the American Consulate only to be met with a calendar that indicated a long four-day holiday weekend ahead. John took Cecil's wishes quite seriously and knew they had to be married at once. He asked to see the consulate judge advocate and they made their plea. Special Judge Nelson Lurton of the U.S. Court for China married them on the spot on November 10, 1938. The wedding dress went unused; Alice was married in a simple suit—no flowers or veil. The couple happily cabled Cecil to let him know she was now Mrs. John Bulkeley. Neither she nor her sister had been able to have the weddings they had dreamed of as young girls.

If the ceremony was not what Alice had expected, the honeymoon was to be an even greater surprise and shock. After the ceremony, the Bulkeleys caught a launch from the former Standard Oil dock along with several young Marines to the *Sacramento*. They boarded the ship just as dinner was being served and dined in the wardroom with the other officers. The meal was simple. Wedding cake and champagne were not on the menu for the evening.

After dinner, John broke the news to Alice that their

first night together would actually be spent apart. He was assigned duty that evening and would have to remain on the ship throughout the night. By this time, she had learned to adjust to the day's surprises. Since night had fallen, it wasn't safe for her to return to the Metropole. But John and several Marines had an alternate plan. They walked Alice over to an abandoned house near the dock, which had been the residence of the Shanghai manager for Standard Oil. They guided her to the basement, which was dimly lit, damp, and cold. In a corner she noticed a small cot and a washroom. The Marines had fashioned a clean little room for her and made their best efforts to make her wedding night as comfortable as possible.

As the men filed out and retreated up the basement stairs Alice, carrying her small purse and wearing the same suit she was married in, embraced her husband with tears of joy. The seriousness of the surrounding danger was not lost on either of them as John reached under his coat and put a cold Colt .45 automatic pistol into her hands "just in case." She had never even held a gun before and now she was putting one under her pillow for the night. She said goodnight to John and tried to put her mind at ease as she lay down on the cot to sleep. Outside, she could hear the Marines pacing back and forth on their patrol, watching for Japanese soldiers, Chinese bandits, and peasant looters. She felt secure that John was among the men protecting her. And now she was his wife and partner in life.

They spent the next few days of a real honeymoon at the Metropole. But within a week of the marriage, John was told by his senior admiral that he had made a terrible mistake in marrying Alice and that his career in the navy was in jeopardy. Other American naval officers also had married Eurasian girls in Shanghai and were told the same thing. Many of these girls were abandoned by their new husbands when their ships sailed; Alice had heard that one girl had taken her own life in despair.

To make matters worse, two months later, the *Sacramento* was ordered to the United States for badly needed repairs. Now John would be on his ship bound for America for the next six months, with plenty of time to reconsider the marriage and have it annulled or just forgotten. Alice realized the terrible dilemma he faced. He loved the navy. It was his whole life and she knew he had a great future and would someday become an admiral. She also knew that he cared for her deeply and wanted to take her to his family and safety in America. They both sensed that soon Japan and Germany would be at war with England and America. Her ancestry—both Japanese and German on her mother's side—would be a problem and would need to be kept secret if they were to stay together.

Understandably, their good-bye was tearful. John promised to send for Alice. Trusting him completely, she allowed him to take on board the *Sacchy* her most treasured possessions so he could have them waiting for her in New York. In eight ornately carved Chinese wooden chests of varying sizes, Alice had carefully packed clothing, linens, items of silver (including a tea set and the hairbrush set Ah-Sim had used to brush out her hair every night), family photographs, letters, and every other item that held special meaning for her.

After John's departure, she went to live with Edith and her family in Hong Kong while she waited for news from America. While she was there, she took her father's advice to avoid a job as an underpaid typist at a petty firm. He cautioned her that naval authorities might have her under observation to see if she was worthy of John. She spent many of her days at a local hospital taking home nursing courses with her mother, who wanted to be of help to her community. The following May, after passing an examination, she and Emily earned certificates from the St. John Ambulance Association. Although she learned many useful skills that would come in handy later in life, her involvement also seemed to help a bit with taking her mind off the long wait for news of John's decision.

In May 1939, when the *Sacramento* finally arrived at the Brooklyn Navy Yard, John immediately sent word to Alice. He asked her to join him as soon as possible and made arrangements for her to sail from Hong Kong to San Francisco on the *President Cleveland* in June. But first she knew she must see her father once more before she left China for the last time and cabled him of her intent to see him.

Her father replied with a cheerful letter. He had arranged free passage for her from Hong Kong to Swatow aboard a Norwegian steamship commanded by a Captain Nilsen. Cecil warned that she may have to sleep on the deck of the ship if it was fully booked, but noted that she would be comfortable. He continued his letter with a request for an eggbeater and a smaller version in a glass jar in order to make mayonnaise. He had been making do with three bamboo sticks tied together since their cook had broken all of the eggbeaters in the house. In closing, Cecil warned Alice not to go near the ship's agents and introduce herself as his daughter, for the "old man still has his uses and one or two kicks left yet."

When Alice arrived at her home with its familiar surroundings, she immediately noticed jagged shards of shrapnel from the bombings that often tore into the house and her mother's beautiful flower garden. The servants by this time had taken to the hills of China's interior, so she and her father had to fend for themselves. They spent their last week together poring over mementoes and talking about the life they had lived in this exotic and beautiful country. Although the atmosphere had a quality of doom, Cecil remained confident that they would all be fine. He clung to his belief that the Japanese would never harm British citizens and felt there was not an urgency for him to escape. The two cooked meals together and once in awhile ventured out to the veranda to survey the harbor, which was now congested with ships. At night they would hear the crack of gunfire and terrible screams, as Japanese soldiers savagely beat the Chinese and routinely gang-raped their women and young girls. During her last days in China, Alice came to realize that John quite possibly was saving her life by taking her out of this part of the world and its current state of brutality.

On the day she was to leave Swatow, Cecil grabbed a bottle of champagne and a small package wrapped in red paper and accompanied Alice to the ship. As they stood on the dock, he poured them each a glass and toasted to Alice's future in America and to the hope that they would someday meet again. Tearfully, she hugged him one last time and his strong arms trembled just slightly. As she began to board the ship, he suddenly remembered the package and placed it in her hands. She thanked him for this parting gift and tucked it safely into her suitcase.

Coats of arms of the Bulkeley and Wood families, both with deep British roots.

John Duncan Bulkeley, Honolulu, June 1935. The young ensign sported the same "fore-and-aft" hat and shoulder boards the night he met Alice aboard the HMS *Diana* in October 1937.

Alice Wood poses in a mandarin-collared dress in her family's garden. Within a few short years, she would have to hide her Eurasian ancestry.

A dedicated amateur photographer, John Bulkeley captured the waterfront glory of Shanghai, ca. 1938. It was the second largest city in the world at the time with a population of 7 million.

Both John and Alice were firsthand witnesses to the atrocities committed in China by Japanese troops in 1937-38. *Above*: A Japanese officer in the act of beheading a Chinese peasant. *Right*: Japanese air raids resulted in death and destruction along a street in Shanghai. Bulkeley's photography was a dangerous practice, but provided gruesome evidence of the occupying force's brutality.

The newly married couple in Shanghai, 1938. The bride's gown stayed in her suitcase and the groom had to leave her alone with a handgun on their wedding night.

Navy Historical Society

The USS *Sacramento* (PG-19) in 1940. The old gunboat was nicknamed "The Galloping Ghost of the China Coast" during its seven years of operations to protect American interests during the Sino-Japanese War. When the ship returned to the Brooklyn Navy Yard for badly needed repairs, aboard was John Bulkeley and eight chests belonging to Alice. (The "*Saccy*" was in Pearl Harbor on Dec. 7, 1941, where she helped rescue survivors of the Japanese attack.)

A rare family moment, 1941.

Elizabeth MacCuaig Bulkeley, John's mother and Alice's staunch wartime companion.

Joan Bulkeley wearing her Victory pin, 1941.

While John made history in the Pacific, Alice waited anxiously by the radio for any news of her husband. Here she is pictured with John Jr. following the news that John had rescued General MacArthur in the Philippines. The New York press frequently cited the family in its wartime articles.

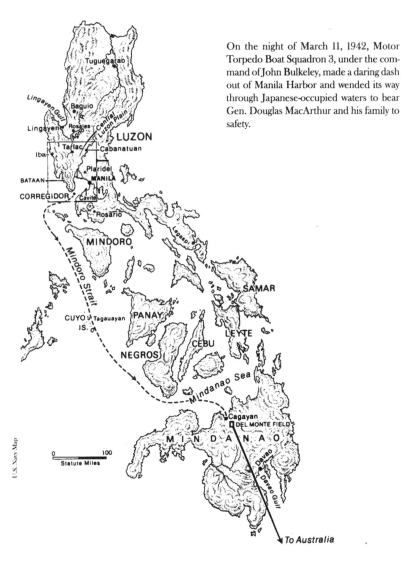

On the night of March 11, 1942, Motor Torpedo Boat Squadron 3, under the command of John Bulkeley, made a daring dash out of Manila Harbor and wended its way through Japanese-occupied waters to bear Gen. Douglas MacArthur and his family to safety.

Fueled by Bulkeley's and others' exploits, PT (patrol torpedo) boats—dubbed the "Mosquito Fleet" by the popular press because of their sting—captured public admiration in the early days of World War II. The sleek, wooden craft stoked enough firepower to sink a battleship and could sneak right up to shore to perform reconnaissance or drop off troops.

Homecoming in Queens, 1942: Lt. John Bulkeley met his new son, John Jr., as (left to right) his mother Elizabeth, nineteen-month-old daughter Joan, and Alice look on. Alice barely had time to explain to her husband that everything was not okay with their second child.

America needed a hero in the dark early days of World War II and John Bulkeley filled the bill. On May 14, 1942, New York City cheered its hero and his attractive young wife.

The New York crowds and tickertape that welcomed John Bulkeley also cheered the other heroes Motor Torpedo Squadron 3, including Lt. Robert Bolling Kelly and Ens. George E. Cox Jr.

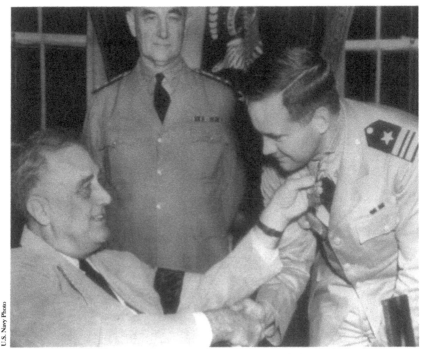

Lt. Comdr. John D. Bulkeley receives the Medal of Honor from President Franklin D. Roosevelt as Vi Adm. Randall Jacobs looks on, 1942.

John Ford's sober, stirring *They Were Expendable* premiered in December 1945, with Robert Montgomery starring as "John Brickley." Alice and John dine with Montgomery (left) and his wife at New York's Stork Club.

A flag-waving Joan Bulkeley stands between her aunt, Leilah Wood, and "Grannie" Emily Wood, on the steps of their Toronto boardinghouse, 1947. After their liberation from Camp Stanley in Hong Kong, Emily, Leilah, and Eric rebuilt their lives in Canada.

As the ship pulled away from the dock for the over-night trip to Hong Kong, Alice was surprised to see a small gathering of some of the family's faithful servants. They had heard of her departure through the grapevine and had decided to risk danger to spend a few last minutes with the Woods, joyfully setting off a string of Chinese firecrackers in farewell.

As Alice's ship took her from the harbor she had known her entire life, she looked around at the Japanese warships that were moored at its entrance. In only a few short days, Swatow would fall and Cecil would find out whether his past work guiding Japanese ships throughout the harbor would ensure that he would receive special treatment when they finally took over his small town. For now, he stood on the pier cheerfully waving to the child who most resembled him both physically and in her bold spirit. How could he ever have imagined back in England that one day his own child would set off for her own dis-tant land in search of a life that held no certain expecta-tions?

From the ship's rail, strong emotions flickered across Alice's face as she watched the figure of her father re-cede. She gathered strength from him until he was but a blurred figure. The rhythmic motion of the sea soothed her nerves; in her mind she knew that she had made the right decision, even though it meant leaving behind the only life she had known. It was so difficult to leave her father. Just then she remembered his package. She sat down on the ship's deck and quickly felt for it in her suit-case. Opening the Chinese red and gold-patterned gift-wrapping paper, she carefully took out a letter written in his fine hand, which all these years had been on so many letters throughout her life—serving as her guiding light. His handwriting had urged her to do her very best at school and had scolded her for spending too much money on makeup.

As she pulled away the paper, she saw a dozen of the most breathtaking embroidered handkerchiefs. Their delicate fabric and stitches were of the most beautiful quality she had ever seen. She held one of the soft squares to her cheek, seeking remembrance, as she read his words:

My dear Alice,

It is an American custom to "root for your own home town." Lest you should have shame for the place where you were born, these exquisite examples of an exquisite art will, I hope, enable you to bear yourself bravely against all contumely of ignorant people. When time shall have given you memories of the yesteryears, I am certain that not least among the gentlefolk whom you have known you will place Ah-Sim, Ah-Kah, Yeong-Kee and his boatmen. Therefore, should China and the Chinese people ever be disparaged in your hearing, tell what you yourself know of them, and take pride in rooting for the place where you were born. Display these handkerchiefs and defy anyplace, anywhere to produce needlework equal to them.

In America the people take you at your own valuation. So, boost yourself, boost your birthplace, boost your nationality and everything else that is yours. But value other people and what they boast of at 5 cents on the dollar.

Your affectionate Father
June 3, 1939

Her eyes began to well up. Brushing the tears away, she went to find her cabin. Within days, Swatow would fall to the Japanese. Alice would never see her father again.

A World Away

CHAPTER SEVEN
1939-1944

Although I try to keep my mind on various interesting subjects, the constant fear of my husband's safety cannot help but penetrate my mind.

Alice Wood Bulkeley's comments to reporters.

Alice and Joan out for a walk in their New York neighborhood.

On the ferry back to Hong Kong, Alice could see the glittering harbor and "the Peak" on Hong Kong Island, a favorite lookout high over the city where lovers made their promises. She made one last round of visits with her family and friends before boarding the American President Lines ship *President Cleveland* for San Francisco. Alice tried to preserve these memories and especially the faces and expressions of her loved ones. As she stood on the deck in the afternoon light, she joined the other passengers who merrily threw paper streamers to the people they were leaving behind on the crowded dock. Below she could see Emily, Leilah, and Edith and Arthur with their young children. Their faces were full of both hope and sadness. Joining in with the other passengers, Alice threw a curly yellow streamer and Edith caught the opposite end. As the ship began to sail, each sister tore a piece off her end, raising it in farewell. Alice folded the small shred of paper into her gloved hand, deciding it would be the last bit of China she would take with her.

It was a sad parting for both sisters. Edith would remain on the dock until the ship was out of view. "I watched the ship depart through the bay," Edith recalled. "I stayed there until it was out of sight. For hours I stood gazing out toward the sea, praying for the Lord to give Alice strength. I prayed for Him to watch over her and one day bring us together again." Edith would later say that she took comfort in the thought that Alice would be safe in America, but it was difficult to imagine her living on the other side of the world. As Alice's ship left the crowded harbor, her eyes took in a fleet of sampans, with their wooden fishing gods to bring good luck, and majestic junks with bright sails. Alice would cherish this memory.

After seven long weeks, the ship finally docked in Honolulu, where swaying hula dancers welcomed the passengers with sweet-smelling flowered leis. The beautiful island setting reminded Alice of her own homeland, but without the violence that had ravaged Swatow. Little did she know that in less than two years the Japanese would launch the surprise attack at Pearl Harbor and that America and the world would be at war.

When she arrived in San Francisco, Alice decided the best place for an overnight stay would be in Chinatown. The sights and smells reminded her of the country she had left and gave her comfort. The following morning, she found her way to the train station and purchased a ticket on a Zephyr streamliner. She then wired her mother-in-law, Elizabeth Bulkeley, about her scheduled arrival in New York City. This sleek train had sleeping cars and a dining car and Alice relaxed as she watched the American landscape change dramatically over the four days of her journey.

Although the trip from China had been long and tiring, in Alice's mind the most anxious part would be meeting Elizabeth MacCuaig Bulkeley. The two women already had corresponded, and Elizabeth had complimented her daughter-in-law by writing that her descriptive and con-cise letter writing revealed a wonderful person. But Alice still harbored some doubts about her own background. Although she had been raised in a very affluent family by American standards, how would John's mother feel about a new daughter-in-law of "questionable" heritage from half a world away? Would she be accepted?

Elizabeth, as a matter of fact, hadn't begun her life in America either. She was of Scottish heritage and was raised in Beaverton, Ontario. While working as an obstetrical nurse at Doctors Hospital in Manhattan, she tended to Frederick Bulkeley, who had contracted a tropical dis-ease in Panama when he was serving in the U.S. Navy. It seems that the patient fell in love with his nurse, whom he called his "Scottish lass." The Tiffany invitations were sent out and the couple was married in New York on Septem-ber 1, 1908.

Frederick's ancestors had a prestigious history in the naval service. Lt. Charles Bulkeley had been second in command of the *Bonhomme Richard* when it defeated the British warship *Serapis* in 1779 in the North Sea, and Midshipman Richard Bulkeley had served with British Lord Horatio Nelson on HMS *Victory*, when Nelson's fleet of twenty-seven ships defeated an armada of thirty-three French and Spanish ships off Trafalgar in 1805.

When Frederick's enlistment in the navy ended, he went into business for himself and later worked for the Electric Boat Company (ELCO) in Bayonne, New Jersey. He and Elizabeth led a pleasant married life, and their son John was born on August 19, 1911, in New York City. His early schooling was in a one-room schoolhouse in Hackettstown, New Jersey. During the first years of his life, John bonded with Frederick's son Chauncey from a previous marriage. To encourage family time together, Frederick purchased a cottage and farm in Millington, New Jersey, as a weekend and summer retreat. Years later, John would place a sign, Mount Olympus, above the door, and plant for his mother her favorite blue-colored hydrangeas.

As a child, John spent countless hours at his father's side, listening to tales of his seagoing ancestors. He taught himself to navigate by the stars and voraciously read books about ships. By the time John was twelve, Frederick signed him on as a seaman aboard the Colombian freighter *Baracoa*, a job that paid a dollar a day. For three summers he sailed mostly in the Caribbean as an employee of the Colombia Steamship Lines.

During the school year, John succeeded in school as a member of the football and track teams, as well as the literary society. Ironically, a speech he gave during his school's Memorial Day observance in 1927 was titled *The War Inevitable.* His senior yearbook correctly predicted that John would one day become a sailor.

The devastating stock market crash of 1929, however, changed everything. Frederick's entire business was lost. In order to survive the Depression, it made sense to sell their primary house and move to the farm so they could live modestly and grow their own food if necessary. John had recently graduated from Hackettstown High School, a one-room school in rural New Jersey, and did not consider remaining on the farm. He was determined to go to sea and sought out an appointment to the U.S. Naval Academy at Annapolis. Initially rebuffed by his own state legislators, he traveled by train to Washington. Since Frederick owned property in Texas, John was able to convince a congressman from that state (where all prospective students had failed the entrance exam) and finally won a Congressional appointment to the academy.

With John at the Naval Academy in Annapolis, Elizabeth and Frederick drifted apart and, finally, separated. Although they never divorced, they never lived together again. Divorce had never been considered, as it was thought to be a disgrace at that time. Frederick eventually recovered financially. Later he met another woman with whom he had a son, but he still loved to visit Elizabeth (the woman he affectionately called "Chick") snappily dressed in a stiff collar, pressed suit and spats.

Alice needn't have worried about meeting Elizabeth, who met Alice's train at Union Station dressed beautifully, her soft gray hair pulled back under a broad-brimmed hat. She was wearing crisp white cotton gloves, a sparkling diamond brooch, and a long, creamy strand of pearls, without which she rarely left the house. She looked up and down at Alice, who was dressed very similarly, and announced with a sweet smile, "You'll do." Immediately struck by her new daughter-in-law's warmth, kindness, and poise, Elizabeth warmly welcomed Alice.

John was still with the *Sacramento* and had returned to the States by way of Europe. He was assisting with the raising of the submarine *Squalas*, but was able to take leave and welcome his bride to New York in June of 1939. At the Commodore Hotel, he filled the room with bouquets of yellow roses. Alice was deeply touched and it was a joyous reunion for them. They were thankful to be together again. At home, an elated Elizabeth bustled about her kitchen in Queens preparing his dinner with all his favorites—fried chicken, mashed potatoes and rich gravy, and homemade apple pie with a mountain of vanilla ice cream.

Settling into her new life in America, Alice realized that she had left her homeland in the nick of time. In July 1939 the Japanese turned their attention to Swatow after pillaging small coastal towns one by one on their way south down the China coast. They bombed the small town severely, killing Chinese soldiers and guerrillas, and terrorizing civilians. In a letter from Edith the same month, she relayed what Cecil was witnessing:

> *...There was one incident of a young girl of 14 years being raped by 10 Japs. This happened in a house near Jardines. The manager complained to the Japanese authorities if they could put a stop to this. They said they could not but that they are getting 100 Japanese prostitutes there and that the Chinese could take their revenge back on their girls. "What are women for anyway?" That is what he said. Isn't it terrible! What a sordid world we are living in today.*

In December 1939 John was assigned to the USS *Saratoga* in Long Beach, California. This meant moving Alice to a two-story, white frame home on Chestnut Avenue.

Since the women had become close, Elizabeth made the move too. And because Alice became pregnant a month later, it was a great support to have Elizabeth there.

Life in Long Beach had a nice sense of normalcy to it for Alice. John was at home, when not on duty aboard ship. The pregnancy went along relatively uneventfully and life continued smoothly. Impressed by Alice's dutiful diary-keeping, John bought a blue, leather-bound, five-year diary of his own. For about two months, he kept records mostly of the progress of hostilities in Europe and how they might affect the United States and, consequently, him. Although he was happy to have Alice with him in their quiet married life, he desperately wanted to be in the center of action, not just on duty in port.

In Kowloon, Emily and Leilah managed on a day-by-day basis, as the Japanese had not yet attacked the crown colony and its British defenders. Leilah was attending the DGS as a "day scholar" and Emily worked as an auxiliary nurse at the local hospital. Edith and her husband Arthur lived nearby with their children. Eric and all able young men, including Alice's old boyfriends, would soon be called up as volunteers to defend Hong Kong. These defenders would later be merged with the British Army and Eric would be given the rank of Corporal.

In June 1940 the government of Hong Kong made the decision to evacuate all of the women and children from the colony, about 3,500 altogether. When Edith heard of this decision on the radio, which they listened to constantly, she did not know where they would be going or for how long. Everyone was ordered to assemble at the Hong Kong ferry terminal. She hastily packed what she thought she would need for herself and May, who was almost four, and baby Richard, who was almost a year old. Leilah would join them as well. Emily would remain at the hospital to help out and wait for news from Cecil.

Arthur drove them all to the pier and there the reality set in. The scene facing them was one of sheer chaos and panic. People were saying their good-byes and elbowing and pushing as they hurried to the ship, with mothers trying to hold onto their children and their luggage. They were finally able to board the ship bound for Australia, where Arthur's family lived. But the ship stopped first in Singapore, where Edith learned about the "Australia White Policy," which banned their entrance to that country because they were considered Eurasian. They were sent on to Manila. The desperate women and children were not able to remain there because of the devastation and were placed with host families in Baguio, farther away. This arrangement was paid for by the Hong Kong government. After a month, the Hong Kong government sent a ship for them to return home. Edith and the children were reunited with Arthur, and Leilah with Emily. For the next year the threat of war was a cloud over the colony of Hong Kong but school for the children, work, and afternoon tea continued, although the conversation was now of war.

On October 1, 1940, Alice gave birth to Joan Isabel, who entered the world feet first. But just as Alice was settling into her southern California home with a new baby, John was already thinking about his career and a change of duty. He had heard about the integral role aircraft carriers would potentially play in the war and seriously considered a career as a navy pilot. John received the approval of the captain of the *Saratoga*, who had been impressed by his lieutenant and encouraged him to pursue his ambitions. He recommended a transfer to flight school in Pensacola, Florida.

New Year's Day 1941 found John, Alice, Elizabeth, and baby Joan driving cross-country. Arriving in New York, Alice set up a new home for her family in a small brownstone apartment in Brooklyn. John left immediately for Pensacola, but not without stopping first in Washington.

This stop would result in a change of plans for John—one that may have changed the course of history and one that would eventually thrust Alice into the limelight of the nation.

The navy was in the beginning stages of creating a new branch of combat crafts, one that would include motor torpedo boats (MTBs or PTs as they would be designated). They were looking for a promising young man to play a leading role and John was a perfect match. He knew immediately that if he refused to take the assignment, it probably would mean an end to promotions in the future, so he put his ideas of flying aside and accepted the assignment. Within a week, he was at the Brooklyn Navy Yard getting the boats ready for action.

Within another few weeks John was headed for Key West, Florida, to conduct antisubmarine trials. Before he left, he passed on to Alice his blue diary, hoping she would put it to better use than he had. As she held it in her hands, she felt like this time, his leaving signaled impending danger. This new assignment on tiny plywood "mosquito boats" seemed to her so much riskier than crossing the waters on a solid ship. Immediately she resumed her diligent practice of keeping a diary. Inside the cover, she created a dedication page with a small photo of herself to symbolically mark her new responsibility.

April 7, 1941

Blue Monday—Everything seems wrong. Near to tears but must keep chin up for John's and Joan's sake.

April 8, 1941

Last day with John before trip to Key West—

awful thought should he never return. Too bad I can't go to be with him. May God bless him always. Joan too will miss him.

John's trials in Key West were a disaster. The sonar units could not withstand the turbulence of a PT boat and all were destroyed. Meanwhile in Washington, Roosevelt had signed the lend-lease bill in response to Germany's defeat of the French army. The new law would suddenly provide a legal way to aid England in the form of ships, tanks, and other weapons (including PT boats) for small payments in return. John was ordered back to New York to prepare the PT boats for the transfer to Great Britain, but on his way discovered the PT's strength: its great endurance on the open water. John was soon to be dispatched to the Philippines as the commander of Squadron 3, a group of six brand-new PTs. They would arrive at Manila Bay on September 28. At the same time, Alice discovered she was pregnant with their second child.

·   ·   ·   ·

Life at home for Alice was like that of many of the military wives in her Brooklyn neighborhood. She spent her days taking care of Joan, studying her law books, visiting Elizabeth and friends, and doing her necessary shopping. Her past lessons in discipline at DGS always served to push her to take on new challenges. For now those challenges included driving an automobile and studying law. It was the automobile that gave her the greatest challenge. Although she took driving lessons, she never quite felt comfortable behind the wheel. In Swatow, all you needed was a rickshaw coolie or a bicycle, not this enor-

mous machine with a will of its own! After failing her initial driving test and even experiencing a minor accident
with Joan in the car where they each bumped the wind-
shield, she doggedly pursued her license. The law classes
seemed easier in comparison.

To make life more comfortable for the entire family,
in August Alice and Elizabeth began looking for an apartment they could share. Although Alice was sad to leave
the comfort of the little neighborhood and the friends she
had made in Brooklyn, the family moved on Joan's first
birthday into a four-room apartment on 41st Street in
Queens. Alice and Elizabeth enjoyed each other's com-
panionship, and this was a way they could wait for news of
John together. Elizabeth also became an enormous help
with Joan as Alice's pregnancy progressed. Although
Elizabeth's sister, Isabel, was frequently on nursing assignments for the infants of wealthy families on Long Island,
she also moved her belongings to the apartment and used
it as her home base. Together the women formed a sort
of unsinkable trio and would support each other through
the good and bad times the next few years would present.

In the evenings, when she wasn't studying, working
toward a certificate in first aid, or serving as the civil defense air raid warden in New York's Sector D, Post 9,
Alice eagerly listened and anxiously waited for reports on
the radio about the situation in Asia. Unlike the other
military wives, she was also listening with hope for good
news about her family so far from her in China. She worried about them, but was able to exchange letters and packages regularly with her mother, and her sisters, Edith and
Leilah, who even sent knitted baby clothes they had made
for "Oscar," as Alice and John referred to the new baby.

In December 1941 the war situation changed not only for Alice's family, but for the entire world. On December 7, the people of Hawaii awakened to a nightmare. The peaceful atmosphere of Pearl Harbor was shattered when the Japanese launched a surprise attack in which 2,388 people were killed and 1,368 were wounded. Twenty-one ships were destroyed or damaged and 169 navy and air force aircraft were demolished. It was the devastating blow that forced the United States to officially enter the war, sending more than one million men to join America's British allies, who had entered the war in 1939. On Christmas Day, Alice learned that Hong Kong, like many of the British, Dutch and American possessions in the Far East, had fallen. That very day in Hong Kong, Japanese propaganda on the radio blared, "A Merry Christmas to the gallant British soldiers...It is time to surrender." A few months later, the package she had sent to her mother with carefully chosen Christmas presents was returned "undeliverable." Now the fate of her entire family was unknown.

Emily, Leilah, Edith and Edith's family were now caught in a "no-win" situation. On December 7, 1941, the day before all volunteers were officially called up and mobilized, Eric came to Edith's home on York Road to say good-bye to her, Arthur, and the children. The news he carried was frightening and grim, as the Japanese were nearing Hong Kong and the volunteers defending the city would be greatly outnumbered. Eric was in a subdued mood and very quiet, even as he played with the children. Edith, ever her jovial self, tried to cheer him and not let on that she was afraid for him and for them all.

The next day, as the family ate breakfast, a torrent of

Japanese planes flew over, dropping bombs with a deafening noise. Billows of thick heavy smoke created a depressing gray haze over the shattered city of Hong Kong. Dust, debris, and ash engulfed the city. The carnage was staggering. The following weeks were chaotic, with the Japanese shelling airfields and looting through the rubble of the collapsed buildings. A blackout was enforced and buildings vibrated, swayed, and collapsed. With sirens blaring and children wailing, residents hurriedly carried glassy-eyed children, still clutching their blankets, into bomb shelters, stepping cautiously to avoid potholes and corpses in the streets. The Japanese penetrated Kowloon first, where the DGS was located, and then flooded the city, plundering, raping, and slaughtering along the way. Japanese street signs replaced Chinese, and the flag of the "Rising Sun" flew at checkpoints and on buildings throughout the city. Water and food would become scarce and later be rationed.

British and Canadian residents were rounded up and forced to open their safety deposit boxes after responding to numbers published in the local paper. The Japanese soldiers gathered the contents, along with other "spoils of war" including home furnishings and plumbing fixtures, and loaded their ships bound for Japan. Meanwhile, the people, who had been held in various places in the city, were ordered on military-type trucks and driven past the inviting and picturesque beaches of Repulse Bay, once a popular spot for lovers, picnics, and a refreshing swim. Now they were on their way to a POW camp.

Emily remained at her post, nursing at the Central British School (CBS), but Edith was unsure of whether her mother had been evacuated or not. With the phone service now inoperable, they could not communicate. By mid-December, Edith and Arthur decided to flee to the Peninsula Hotel with Leilah and the children. Edith packed a small suitcase and borrowed a car. A neighbor and her son came along. As Arthur drove through the war-torn and deserted streets, they noticed Japanese flags flying from every building.

Suddenly a Japanese patrol stopped the car, pulled Arthur out and made him put his hands up and walk to other side of the road. With Leilah at her side, baby Richard in her arms, and May clinging to her skirt, Edith fought to control her fear and emotions despite feeling a spreading weakness overcoming her. Swiftly and savagely, the Japanese took Arthur and the neighbor's son away and ordered the women to go home on foot. Without her husband, suitcase and car, Edith was numb and almost paralyzed with fear. Her legs were trembling as she and her neighbor left the scene with the frightened children in tow. She would not see Arthur until the next month.

Arthur and nine other men were forced into a gutter with their hands tied behind their backs. They sat there for six hours in the hot sun while the soldiers took turns hitting them on the head with the butts of their rifles. One soldier would put a cigarette in each man's mouth and then another soldier would come by and brusquely knock it out. They were marched to a filthy Chinese school where they resorted to drinking water from an unused goldfish tank and were later transferred to the Kowloon Hotel.

With only a purse and passport, Edith and the others in the little group walked down the road as if in a dream. The people were indistinguishable from each other as they fled. When they finally arrived at their home, Chinese looters were ransacking their house. Desperate, they decided to walk to the hospital where Emily worked. Along the way, three Chinese bandits attacked them, taking Edith's last possession—her purse. Leilah ran with the children to the CBS and fortunately found Emily there. Edith arrived a few minutes later, shaking with terror, and they all stayed together as the Japanese took over the hospital less than a half-hour later.

After brief stays at the CBS and the Kowloon Hospital they were taken to the Chinese YMCA building. Through all of this confusion, Arthur miraculously managed to have love letters secretly delivered to Edith. In these letters, which were delivered by strangers, he encouraged her to stay strong, writing in one, "Love eternal burns forever. Time and space makes no omission." In another, he wrote, "How many tongues, how many lips are praying to the Almighty and beseeching Him to end this. Will our prayers and their prayers be answered?" These words gave her the encouragement she needed and the heart to survive.

Arthur's moving words served to calm Edith somewhat and get her through each day. But not only was she struggling to protect her children and herself in the midst of a war zone, she also had to protect them from the illnesses that resulted from living in such abhorrent conditions. During their stay at the YMCA, Richard, almost three and eagerly looking forward to his birthday cake, suddenly came down with a high fever and convulsions. Fortunately, Edith was able to convince a Japanese guard to take her child to a doctor at the hospital across the road. Little May, her eyes frozen with fear, remained with her grandmother and watched as another scene unfolded in front of them. Japanese guards killed a civilian and dumped

the poor man's body into a wheelbarrow. Such occur-
rences had now become common. The deafening bombing also continued to make them nervous and afraid. The
best news of all was that Richard recovered.

About a month later, the family was finally reunited
with Arthur and were transferred to Stanley Camp, which
was the site of Stanley Prison and St. Stephen's College
(which still exists today). The St. Stephen's library was used
as a hospital and became a gruesome scene for about 100
wounded British and Canadian volunteers who were mas-
sacred by drunken Japanese soldiers on Christmas day.
Two doctors were killed and the nurses raped. At the far
end of the lush Stanley peninsula, the flag of "The Rising
Sun" waved over the encampment of the Japanese soldiers. The internees were given only one meal a day: rice
and watery soup. Fortunately, Emily had retained her ability to speak some Japanese and was able to prevent the
guards from raping the young girls. Little May was no
longer the carefree youngster, but silent. Her eyes were
joyless.

The first six months at Camp Stanley were the worst
for the Wood family. They were surrounded by barbed
wire and, as there was only one road in and out of the
camp, escape was hardly possible. Edith's small children
had already seen the horrors that war can bring. As Edith
pondered about this, she tried to protect and comfort them
as best she could with stories, games, and songs. Protecting their physical health was another concern. With little
to eat, Edith picked out the mice droppings from the
children's rice bowls in their packed housing in Bungalow A that they shared with forty-five people of all ages
and backgrounds. Almost all slept on the wooden floors.

As food became even more scarce, the prisoners resorted to eating anything they could find or grow. Later on they were able to keep a small garden where, to their delight, the seeds from a tin of canned tomatoes miraculously sprouted into tomato plants. Once or twice a year, the International Red Cross was able to send in care packages with a few supplies, including clothing, tins of food, peanuts, sugar, and powdered milk. Many internees suffered from beriberi, sores that were slow to heal, loss of memory, temporary blindness, and forgetfulness. Most prisoners, including the Wood family, suffered from malaria and dysentery.

For nearly four years, they would suffer malnutrition and abhorrent living conditions. Emily's diamond rings, smuggled into the camp sewn into a leather pouch in her brassiere, alleviated some of the hunger when some were traded in the camp's black market. Some guards would look the other way when the camp's residents would "break the rules." But others would execute a person for little cause. The once spunky British and Canadian defenders were now defeated and were forced to march past the barbed wire fences of Camp Stanley. Edith saw them and wept. The camp cemetery began to fill up with crudely made rough wooden crosses. Life on the outside of the camp wasn't much better and the prisoners resigned themselves to camp life.

As time passed and their imprisonment became a reality of years, not months, the prisoners became well-organized and the camp began to function like a small town. Imprisoned doctors formed a small "hospital" with instruments made from bits of a ceiling fan. To retain a sense of "normalcy" for the children, prisoners formed a camp school, where the children attended lessons and progressed through grade levels even though paper was a rare commodity. Leilah managed to earn merit badges in the camp's Girl Guides program, run by the prisoners. Even items normally taken for granted in everyday life had to be jury-rigged. When Leilah outgrew her shoes, Emily fashioned a "new" pair using pieces of wood from a door, scraps of felt from an old hat for the lining, and bits of a discarded tire for the soles. Knowing how much Leilah, a young and sensitive girl, would be comforted with some toys, Edith collected scrap material and fashioned a small rag doll for her young sister and a tea set from tin cans.

Leilah also managed to keep an embroidered purse with a few silver dollars. Whenever the Japanese guards made an inspection, Leilah put the purse into the pocket of the only outfit she had to wear, and Emily told the guard that Leilah had some candy. Emily took special care to keep the thirteen-year-old girl's blond locks cropped, so the guards would think she was younger and wouldn't rape her.

Far away in Japan, Alice's brother Eric was being held as a POW in Osaka. With barely enough food to avoid starvation, he and the other prisoners endured forced hard labor, which included building bridges for the enemy and working in mines. Suffering physically from rickets and poor vision brought on by starvation, Eric also endured mental torture and the emotional uncertainty of not knowing the whereabouts of his family. Despite being discouraged and downhearted, he summoned up his strength and prayed to God that they would ultimately prevail and survive. He felt that surely God had a plan for them.

As each day passed with no news from her family or of John, Alice became increasingly worried and desperate for any word of their fate. Sundays were the worst, followed by what she termed "Blue Mondays." For her, Sundays had always been a family day, first in Swatow and later with John. Not hearing from him was heartbreaking for her. His last letter had arrived December 7. She knew nothing of his heroics in saving nearly 200 civilians after their inter-island steamship, the SS *Corregidor*, struck a mine and sunk in Manila Bay on December 17. More than 1,000 men, women, and children were on board. John had heard the tremendous explosion rock his camp, and he and his men rushed out aboard three PT boats to reach the scene. His boat alone, which had been built to hold eleven men, took aboard 196 oil-soaked survivors. Two hundred and ninety-six people were rescued on three boats. "The miracle of the loaves and fish has been repeated," John said afterward.

On January 20, Alice's daily routine was interrupted by a reporter for the *Daily News,* who called with news that John had sunk a 5,000-ton Japanese ship in Subic Bay in the Philippine Islands. Immediately reporters, telegrams and phone calls poured in and her life was turned upside-down. Paramount and Universal movie people swarmed the apartment with their cameras, craving a story that would raise the morale of the country with a hometown hero. Alice was bombarded with requests for appearances at events to support the war effort and accepted those she felt would help. As her delivery date drew near, however, she found herself increasingly fatigued and had to decline many of the invitations.

On March 23, Alice received a call from a reporter

for the *Long Island Star* calling to ask how she felt about her husband's heroism in the Pacific. As he filled her in on the details of her husband's daring rescue of General MacArthur through the Japanese blockade surrounding Corregidor, her heart swelled with tremendous pride for her husband, who always seemed to be in the right place to change and to save lives. The media once again swarmed around Alice and Elizabeth, seeking any tidbit of information that would make Americans feel that they knew this American hero, this brave man who seemed to be making enormous headway with this war against the treacherous Japanese. Although she obliged willingly, her old fears about her ancestry came back to the surface. What if the media wanted too much information about her? Here John was killing "the evil Japs" and the world was bracing against Germany's Hitler, and she carried the blood of both of these nations.

.   .   .   .

In a cold, dark room on a gray metal cot in Shanghai, Cecil listened to radio San Francisco. John Duncan Bulkeley—the man he had allowed to sweep his daughter to safety in America—was a hero. He was grateful that Alice was safely ensconced in a new life in America, but there were nights Cecil openly wept in despair for his own life and the uncertainty of the fate of his wife and remaining children. He had made such a fulfilling life for his family in this country, so far away from his home in England. Everything he had worked so hard to build was gone—his dear family, his beautiful home and furnishings, his boats, and even the valuable paperwork that proved his ownership of property. Now he was alone with only a small bag of personal items. The Japanese had taken everything from him—everything but his strong faith in God and his steadfast dignity.

Cecil and other British colonists had been under house-arrest by the Japanese for a month when the enemy decided it would make escape more difficult if they moved the men to Kakchiohm across from the town side of Swatow. Cecil was locked up in the British Consulate. At the end of April, Cecil and thirty-three other men were crowded into the No. 3 hold of a filthy Japanese freighter with only what they could carry after repeatedly being robbed and looted. Cecil confided to a friend, John Liley of Butterfield & Swire, that he was leaving half his life behind. Thirty years of Cecil's work had vanished overnight, Liley recalled in a 1943 letter to Alice.

> *At first he wanted to stay and see things through but the Gendarmes made future conditions so impossible and so threatening that he wisely joined the "No-Shirt Party" and came along with the gang, and I can assure you, Alice, that he did the correct thing.*

Cecil and John Liley shared adjoining beds in the Columbia Country Club in Shanghai where they were held with others by the Japanese. There they gazed at the spectacle of the American eagle spreading its wings beneath a "poached-egg" [Japanese] flag, Liley wrote. Their diet consisted mostly of yams.

> *He remained surprisingly active for his years, though, I must say his face revealed the fact that he*

seemed to be ageing very considerably, and I sus-
pected that he did at times weep in the darkness. But
this, Alice, in any case, is nothing of which to be
ashamed. Talking with him sometimes he reminded
me of what someone, I forget whom, once wrote of
Lincoln—"It seemed in his later years as though the
knuckles of sorrow had pushed his eyes deep into
their sockets." He was obviously full of principle, reso-
lution and fight.

Although other men chose to leave Shanghai (Liley fled to Bombay) when the Japanese gave them the chance, Cecil chose to stay in order to try to get word on Emily and the girls, which was next to impossible. Meanwhile, Cecil's living conditions continued to worsen. Surrounded by barbed wire and disease, he managed to survive at times on one shriveled sweet potato a day. Food was rationed and was often weevil-infested. Dysentery and malnutrition, which led to heart disease in many prisoners, were common. Although there was a small school for the children run by missionaries and an entertainment committee, the severity of the situation was evident at the camp hospital where the POWs suffered from beriberi, malaria and pneumonia; patients were put on half rations, as they were expected to die anyway.

·   ·   ·   ·

On March 29, Alice received a cable from John telling her that he was okay. Although all reports from the media told her he was still well and fighting, it was so good to hear directly from him and such a considerate thing for him to do. What she didn't learn was how desperate John's situation had become—that he and his men were on the verge of starvation, their base of operations destroyed and, along with it, their supplies, including fuel. Nearly one-third of the Filipino population had fled to the mountains to find refuge from the Japanese bombardments and attacks. Yet John knew he had been lucky: less than one month after he evacuated General MacArthur and Philippine President Manuel Quezon, the American and Filipino forces left behind were captured by Japanese troops and forced to begin the pitiless ninety-mile march—known ever after as the Bataan Death March—that 20,000 men would never complete.

On April 3, Alice suddenly went into labor with her second child, which she knew would be another breech birth. Even with Elizabeth and Isabel there for support, she felt completely on her own. Every member of her family was now a prisoner of the Japanese. And what would become of John, who was in the middle of one of the most dangerous parts of the world? Would he even live to see this baby?

To add to her challenging world, John Duncan Bulkeley, Jr. was born with numerous physical and mental handicaps. She not only had to learn a whole new way of life caring for this pitiful and frail child, but she had to hide his condition from a hungry media circus that wanted photographs of the new hero's son. The news media were kind to her and respected her wishes when she showed them John Jr. They reported nothing about his condition.

In John's five-year diary, which she took over in April 1941, she recorded her daily efforts to get Johnny to nurse and her despair at hearing his muffled whimpers. Her last entry was on April 21, 1942. Alice would never keep another diary, whether from lack of time or sheer sadness of many moments. But she would later write selected family stories for her children.

.   .   .   .

On May 8, the United Airlines Mainliner rolled to a stop at New York's LaGuardia Airport. Alice's first glimpse of John surprised her, as he had lost thirty pounds in the past few months. John told the throng of reporters that right now his wants were simple: "A little rest, a little home life and plenty of Mom's home cooking." Alice did manage to tell him during a quick embrace for the cameras that the baby was not okay. The newsmen caught John's confused expression only slightly as he pulled away, craving more information than Alice could immediately give him.

The following days were exhausting and sleepless, with every minute filled with events. John spoke to thousands of people, encouraging them to support the war effort and not to let their "boys" down. He visited the Electric Boat Company (ELCO) in Bayonne, New Jersey, where the engines for the PT boats were manufactured, and told the workers how their work at home had made an enormous difference in the Pacific. The young couple even experienced the thrill of a New York ticker-tape parade to honor John and his surviving officers, with a record number of people gathered on the parade route or leaning out building windows along the route to wave, blow kisses, and shower the men in shredded telephone-book confetti and flowers. Kitty Carlisle presented orchids to John, saying, "You know that an orchid epitomizes the greatest praise we New Yorkers can pass out." Alice received a bouquet of roses and orchids. The program following the parade included Jimmy Dorsey and His Orchestra, Danny Kaye, and Jane Froman, among others.

During this time, John was approached by representatives of Joseph Kennedy, Sr. A meeting was arranged between the Bulkeleys and Kennedy at New York's Plaza Hotel, where Kennedy asked John to nominate his second son, John Fitzgerald, to enter the PT boat program. John agreed to interview the young man in Chicago and found that he had the background, education, experience, and fearlessness required. John nominated John F. Kennedy, and JFK proved what his father had predicted to John Bulkeley: "I think that one day you will look back and realize that ours was a meeting of destiny today."

In the White House, President Roosevelt was preparing to present John with the Medal of Honor for his extraordinary heroism in the Philippines. This honored medal, the highest award the United States can bestow on an individual, is reserved for members of the armed forces who have scaled the heights of courage at the risk of their lives above and beyond the call of duty. Alice had always known that John had within him this inherent courage, strength, and character, which would impel him to save his fellow man.

For John, the meeting would focus less on his past accomplishments and more on the future of the war. MacArthur had given him specific instructions. He was to explain how American soldiers in the Philippines had been sacrificed by their country, and left to die or be bayoneted by the thousands along the route of the Bataan Death March. Many were interned afterward among the 8,000 people in the largest POW camp in Asia. They had hoped that help would come but, sadly, none came. MacArthur now wanted John to urge Roosevelt to send the necessary troops and weapons to Australia so MacArthur could build an army and retake the Philippines.

On the morning of August 4, 1942, Alice and John reached the imposing White House gates for the scheduled ceremony, but because John didn't have a written invitation, the guard called the president's office. Two staff members came out to greet the Bulkeleys and then gave Alice the crushing news—she would not be admitted inside. John would receive his medal without her.

Stunned, Alice said good-bye to John as he rushed inside and turned away from the gates. Her first thought was to go for a walk in Lafayette Park across the street. As she slowly sat down on a park bench, all she could conclude was that a background check by the president's staff must have revealed her background. How could they allow a woman who was part Japanese and German to enter the Oval Office?

As her eyes began to swell with tears, she remembered her father telling her, "Head up, chin out" and, taking a deep breath, she opened her pocketbook to reach for a handkerchief. Instead of her usual white-linen one, she pulled out one of the exquisite handkerchiefs her father had given her as she sailed from Swatow for the last time. She had brought it for good luck from New York. Opening the folds, she gazed at the intricate work and couldn't help but remember Father's eloquent words urging her to be proud of her heritage. His words seemed so simple as she read them from his letter the first time. But now they rang with a stinging irony.

As the sun rose over the Washington capital, Alice,

with puffy eyes, sat on the hard bench remembering the simpler, less-complicated days of her childhood in the balmy climate of Swatow. When she finally realized she had been daydreaming, she stood up and began to make her way back to the unfriendly gates. Although she didn't know it at the time, the ceremony for John was also a tactical move, allowing the president to surreptitiously invite John back to his office that night, where John would deliver a stinging request for Roosevelt's support in front of a shocked staff.

John didn't know it at the time, but the Allies had made the firm resolve to win the war in Europe before focusing on the Far East.

Back at home, John's dream of his son following in his footsteps was dashed. He held the baby tensely, worried that any small movement would lead to more damage. Earlier, in front of the news media, he had said, "He's grand. He gets a Navy 'E' for excellence." But he was concealing his grief, wondering how this could be the greatest and most difficult time of their lives together all at once?

After a few months of appearances, war bond rallies, and visits to shipyards and factories to inspire Americans in the fight against the enemy, John was sent back to sea. In the Southwest Pacific, he took command of Motor Torpedo Boat Squadron 7 and took part in the Battle of Bismarck Sea, the invasion of the Trobriand Islands, and conducted the naval blockade of the Vitiaz Strait. He met every mission with bravery and valor. In late 1943 he reported to the European theater, where he led PT Task Group 102, running espionage agents and French Resistance fighters into the Normandy and Brittany coasts. Later he commanded all American MTB squadrons in England.

Meanwhile, Alice was at home, managing against all odds to mainstream Johnny in a world that wasn't quite ready to accept a child who was so different. Her days were consumed with his care, and she also managed to get letters to her family in China. But the news she received from that part of the world became increasingly tragic. In January of 1943, she received a letter from her Swatow friend Duggie:

> *As Kitty is also writing, I am leaving your girl-friends to her and just confine my news to your male friends. As you probably know we were almost all of us in the Volunteers so prepare for a bit of bad news.*
> *1. Donald was killed, shot in the head about 21st Dec.*
> *2. Ernie Zimern is missing believed killed and has been from 19th Dec.*
> *3. Andrew Zimern was the first in his battery (5th A.A.) to be killed.*
> *4. Poor George Lau is also missing believed killed; he and Ernie were with me in a position and while I was in the lucky half who got away they weren't heard of again.*
> *5. Tinker is O.K. He is a prisoner of war. For a month about April last he was in the hospital with a stomach ulcer.*

The letter continued with descriptions of her old friends and their respective fate and closed by commending John's bravery and heroism: "I have never met your husband but I have heard since of all he's done. You ought to be very proud. Thank him for me for at least giving the Japs a dose of what's coming to them for their misdeeds. Our boys need avenging."

Howard Chandler Christy's dramatic portrait of John Bulkeley, painted from life after World War II, looks down upon visitors to the Naval Academy in Annapolis.

Alice and John aboard the USS *Rochester*, a heavy cruiser, during the early 1950s when John was based in Long Beach, California.

Left: Capt. John Bulkeley extends a firm handshake to the young man he had personally recommended into the PT boat training program—President John F. Kennedy, 1961. *Top*: After President Kennedy promoted him to admiral, Bulkeley's strong hand successfully countered Fidel Castro's designs on the U.S. Naval Base in Guantanamo, Cuba.

At "Gitmo" Alice and John enjoy a rare outing aboard the *Drumbeat*, the sailboat that John built. After just one outing with Admiral Bulkeley, some friends declined future invitations; he sailed his boat with the same gusto displayed in other areas of his life.

Alice never really needed to borrow the admiral's cap to show that she was, as John affectionately called her, "The Boss." This photograph was taken in October 1994 in Virgina Beach, Virginia.

Bronze busts of Admiral Bulkeley by Ann La Rose can be found at the Naval Academy, the Navy War College, and the Naval Amphibious Base. It is also on board the USS *Bulkeley*.

John and Alice enjoyed attending reunions each year. In September 1995 they attended a USS *Endicott* reunion in Washington, D.C., with daughter Joan.

Alice celebrated her sixtieth birthday surrounded by her children. Pictured, from left, Diana, John Jr., Gina, Alice, Peter, and Joan.

Joan and Herb Stade settled in Oak Brook, Illinois. Shown here at their daughter's wedding are (left to right) Herb, Samantha (Krill), Joan, Shari, Tom Hense, Karen, Tyler (Krill), and Karen's husband, Scott Krill.

John Jr., pictured here playing the piano for his parents, served as the organist for the Washington Navy Yard chapel for twenty-two years. The model sitting atop the family piano is of John's legendary *PT 41*.

Peter and Carol Bulkeley live in Virginia Beach, Virginia. Pictured (left to right) are Lauren, Peter, Carol, and Christopher.

Gina and Steven Day live in Nebraska with their two children. Pictured (clockwise from top) are Steven, Gina, John, and Jennifer.

Diana and her husband Harvey live near Alice in Maryland. Pictured (left to right) are Kelley, Harvey, Diana, and Shannon.

Vice Admiral John Duncan Bulkeley was interred at Arlington National Cemetery with full military honors on April 19, 1996. Alice can be seen to the left of the headstone carrying a large bouquet of yellow roses, which she placed on John's grave.

On June 24, 2000, Alice was joined by many women of the Bulkeley family for the christening ceremonies of the USS *Bulkeley* in Pascagoula, Mississippi. Pictured (left to right) are Sarah Fargo (Navy representative), Carol Bulkeley, Diana Lindsay, Gina Day, Joan Stade, and Comdr. Carlos Del Toro, captain of the *Bulkeley*.

A personal moment for Alice at the christening of the USS *Bulkeley*.

Alice is passing her love for the sea on to succeeding generations. Pictured here during a cruise to Alaska in 2001 are Alice with her great-grandchildren, Tyler Stade Krill (left) and Samantha Alison Krill.

Diana and Terry
Heuman, 2018.

Four Generations. Joan, Alice,
Karen, and Samantha during a
cruise to Alaska, 2001.

Peter and Rebecca Bulkeley, 2017.

USO Gala at the Navy Pier in Chicago, October 19, 2009.

Alice and John Bulkeley and Family, 1992. Top row (standing; left to right): Herb, Joan, Shari, Scott, Karen, Gina, Steve, John. Bottom row (sitting; left to right): John, Diana, Harvey, Kelly, Shannon, Alice, John, Jennifer, Chris, Lauren, Carol, and Peter.

Summer 2019. Top row (left to right): Scott Krill, Tom and Shari Hense, Samantha, Karen, and Tyler Krill. Bottom row (left to right): Tommy Hense, Joan and Herb Stade with Emilia and Eric Hense.

John, too, suffered the loss of many comrades in arms. He knew and mourned the loss of these valued friends, but would only learn at the war's end just how many had died: from his original Motor Torpedo Boat Squadron, only twenty-nine of its 113 men survived the war.

Only a few months later, toward the end of May, Alice would get the most crushing news of the war. After returning home from a visit with John's brother Chauncey in Albany, New York, she found an envelope from the Foreign Office in London. As she tore open the official-looking envelope and read the first lines, she could feel her entire body fall apart from the inside:

Madam,

I am directed by Mr. Secretary Eden to inform you with regret that the Swiss representative in Shanghai, who is in charge of the interests of British subjects in occupied China, has reported the death of Captain Cecil Herbert Wood at Shanghai on the 26th March, 1943.

A world away in Camp Stanley, Emily would take Leilah for a walk. Near the camp cemetery she broke the sad news that she had received. Emily had had a vivid dream the night before. In it, she saw her husband being taken to a small house on the waterfront and led upstairs into a back room. She heard the words "Asama Manu," which was the name of a Japanese ship, and then heard the sound of a shot being fired. She woke up in terror and realized that her husband was dead and prayed for him. Alice did not learn until much later that one out of every four captives of the Japanese perished.

The news of her father's death, which she had so feared, was a reality. Her father was gone. She clung to her faith in God, which had been instilled in her so long ago by her parents and at St. Andrew's Church. It would take the full force of that faith to get her through the next few years.

Aftermath

CHAPTER EIGHT
1946-1950

Each morning when I wake I say,
"I place my hand in God's today",
I know He'll walk close to my side
My every wandering step to guide,
He leads me with the tenderest care
When paths are dark and I despair—
No need for me to understand
If I but hold fast to His hand.

Florence Scripps Kellogg
Part of a poem a woman handed to
Alice at Johns Hopkins Hospital
during one of her son's surgeries.

A portrait from 1946.

In March 1944 John was assigned to the European Theater to head up PT operations in the English Channel. He was based in Dartmouth, England, and his PTs carried out dangerous nighttime operations under harrowing conditions between England and German-occupied France. They had to pass through German convoy lanes and minefields while avoiding detection by German radar. Off the beaches of northern France, the PTs would anchor and put ashore incoming agents, and pick up the returning agents. John and his crew went on these missions unarmed, as they were posing as an air and rescue operation. John had started out with three boats, but sixty-seven additional boats were ordered to England and were berthed at Portland, Dartmouth, and other areas. John was the task group commander and was ordered to hunt the menacing German E-boats, oversized versions of PT boats. On June 1, John took command of all PT boat operations involving D-Day and his critical mission was to clear the sea lanes for the Allied Invasion of Normandy.

On D-Day, June 6, 1944, John led sixty-seven PTs and 110 minesweepers to prepare the Baie de LaSeine area for the arrival of the assault force that would land on the beaches of Normandy. On D-Day, John was aboard

PT-504 when the USS *Cory* hit a mine. He and his PT boat crews rescued the men. On D-Day plus one, the USS *Tide*, a minesweeper, was ripped apart by a mine, and John was there to pull the men onto his boat while using a megaphone to give out orders. All the while, the *Tide* was in danger of exploding. Knowing that her husband would be in great danger, Alice had tucked in John's uniform pocket a copy of Psalm 91, which reads in part: "A thousand shall fall at thy side, and ten thousand at thy right hand, but it shall not come nigh thee."

By 1944, when he assumed command of the USS *Endicott* (a destroyer assigned to the invasion of southern France), he had received almost every medal the United States had to offer, some more than once. On the *Endicott*, John once again managed against all odds to sink two German corvettes after a running gunfight and took on board nearly 200 German prisoners of war. In 1945, legendary movie director John Ford would make the movie *They Were Expendable,* based on John's heroics in the Philippines. The movie starred John Wayne, Robert Montgomery (in John's role), Donna Reed, and Ward Bond.

In the forward for W. L. White's book, *They Were Expendable*, the author wrote the following about John and his men:

> *I have been wandering in and out of wars since 1939, and many times before have I seen the sad young men come out of battle—come with the whistle of flying steel and the rumble of falling walls still in their ears, come out to the fat, well-fed cities behind the lines, where the complacent citizens always choose*

from the newsstands those papers whose headlines proclaim every skirmish as a magnificent victory. And, through those plump cities the sad young men back from battle wander as strangers in a strange land, talking a grim language of realism which the smug citizenry doesn't understand, trying to tell of a tragedy which few enjoy hearing. These four young men differ from those I have talked to in Europe only in that they are Americans, and the tragedy they bear witness to is our own failure, and the smugness they struggle against is our own complacency.

With a gunshot to his head in his Berlin bunker on April 30, 1945, Adolph Hitler finally ended his reign of terror over Europe. As the world waited to see the Japanese brought to their knees, the full extent of the atrocities of war became clear throughout Europe and Asia. Alice began to feel the war's full impact on her life as well —not only on her family in China, but also on her immediate family, specifically John.

In July 1945 John reported to the Bethlehem Steel Corporation's yards in Staten Island, New York, to oversee the completion of the navy's newest destroyer, the *Stribling*, destined for action in the Pacific. He was just a New York borough away from his growing family, still residing in Queens, but only able to rejoin them infrequently during leaves. The war still raged in the Pacific, with the Japanese military mounting a fierce and desperate resistance in spite of a defeat that was now all but inevitable. Since John had not seen combat action since returning to the United States aboard the *Endicott* earlier in the year, he was thrilled to be given command of this modern destroyer and eager to get under way and see more action. For the birth of his third child on July 20, John was close by—if not on hand—for the arrival of Peter Wood Bulkeley, who joined five-year-old Joan and three-year-old John, Jr., in the cramped Queens apartment.

Peter's birth coincided with a time of significant trial for the young Bulkeley family. This was certainly not an uncommon occurrence in the continuing wartime atmosphere, but an unusual combination of divisive forces threatened to pull the young couple apart. For John, his character was challenged by not only the grim and brutal necessities of war, but fame as a war hero as well. Alice faced the daunting challenge of raising a mentally handicapped child, and two other children, in a new country and with minimal resources. She was also continuing to seek information on the fate of her family in Hong Kong and was very worried about them.

Little did Alice know that at Camp Stanley, Emily and Edith were struggling to keep their children alive. On July 25, 1945, an unmarked plane dropped numerous ammonia bombs on the camp. These bombs are designed to explode upon contact with water. While Edith and Arthur were away from their bungalow and Emily stayed with the children, one of these bombs landed in the bathroom of their bungalow, into the filled bathtub. Upon their panicked return to the bungalow, Edith and Arthur discovered that May, Richard, and Leilah had been hurt, the two girls seriously. Leilah had been reading to the children when the bomb hit. Richard, who was sitting in his grannie's lap, was thrown outside by the force of the blast. Edith and Arthur found him in the arms of a fellow prisoner in a state of bewilderment. Emily was covered in blood and in shock but, miraculously, only badly bruised. Her real concern was for the children and their injuries.

Leilah and May were unconscious, having borne the tremendous impact of the explosion. Their bodies were ashen, lifeless, and bloodied by flying debris. Two men found them and carried them to the makeshift hospital, where doctors removed the imbedded fragments from their arms. After many weeks they recovered, but the emotional scars were deep. They were even more apprehensive, nervous and quiet. The loss of their childhood was evident in their eyes, which asked, "Why?" Edith prayed for their health and also that freedom would come soon.

Back in New York, wartime coverage of the young hero papered over the challenges facing the young family. "That makes me quite a staff, counting Admiral Jasper," John had quipped about his growing family to reporters covering the *Stribling*, a new destroyer weighing 2,250 tons, at the steel plant. (Admiral Jasper was the family cat.) On that particular day, John wore eighteen ribbons topped by the Medal of Honor. At age thirty-five, he already ranked among the most decorated fighting men in U.S. history, and he remained intensely focused on rising through the ranks to achieve his career goal—the two stars of an admiral.

The press never profiled the fate of another family pet, John's beloved dog, Penny. Alice wrote it down, however, and it bears repeating as a parable of the challenges that John was facing during that time. Penny was a Marine-trained dog that John had nursed back to health in 1943 after she had been injured and left to die on the Japanese-occupied South Seas island of Bougainville.

When John went to England in 1944 to prepare for D-Day, Penny went with him and became a mascot. In the summer of 1945, during the transition between the *Endicott* and the *Stribling*, she came to live with the Bulkeley family, and became quite attached to Alice and the children. No one knew that Penny, like Alice, was also pregnant. Alice wrote:

In the wee early morning hours of July 20th, the labor pains started, and I got up and paced the bedroom floor, trying to keep track of the pain. Penny was beside me, and paced the room with me...It all happened very fast, and Peter Wood Bulkeley arrived at 6 a.m....John was away on Navy assignment, and we had a hard time getting in touch with him. I stayed in the hospital just a couple of days, as all went well and I was in good shape. Meanwhile, Penny had delivered four beautiful puppies in my closet when I was gone. So on my return home, she was there to greet me at the door, wagging her tail, and sniffing the bundle (my baby) that I was carrying. She then led me to the closet to show me her puppies. It was a wonderful experience. I only wish John could have been there to see it. He did not know he had a pregnant dog. So like him to spring surprises on me.

When it came time to move the puppies, however, Penny bared her teeth and moved to attack Elizabeth. John soon returned to meet his newborn son, to see Penny and her puppies (which all found good homes with families in the Bulkeley's Queens neighborhood), and to board his new ship and take Penny with him. The incidents increased and Penny became again the wartime guard dog that she had been trained to be—culminating in her attack on two workmen, who had entered John's cabin in the skipper's absence. Penny had to be destroyed, and John would do it himself. He joined Penny in his cabin aboard the ship for the last time, took out his .45, said good-bye to Penny, and shot her.

How was John to reconcile the guerrilla—a man who had had to kill a German soldier with his bare hands on a beach in Normandy to keep him from raising a general alarm—with the family man? The war itself had brought out a "seek and kill the enemy" instinct, something a person like John was not comfortable with, even though it meant self-preservation. The guilt would always be there. By 1945, John was a thoroughly trained warrior: he had fought in the treacherous Pacific and then crossed to the Atlantic for the final drive to end the war in Europe. Even now, as commanding officer of the *Stribling*, he was eager to launch back into the Pacific for his third crack at the Japanese military machine.

But President Harry S. Truman had other plans.

Less than two weeks after Peter's arrival, the first two atomic bombs were unleashed on Japan, and the guns fell silent all across the Pacific. Although the vast war had already ended in Europe, the complete surrender of Japan—presided over by General MacArthur no less—had to have been a remarkable moment for both John and Alice. It must have been hard, initially, for either of them to comprehend that complete victory was truly at hand, as their courtship and wedding had been set against a bloody backdrop of Japanese aggression. Both had witnessed the relentless, pitiless, barbaric, implacable nature of the Japanese military. But now, the young husband and wife joined the rest of the world, after more than seven years of escalating hostilities, in a collective sigh of relief and the joy of being a family again.

In the aftermath of any war, the final battle is waged on the home front. Life on Long Island had become enormously challenging, and in the Bulkeleys' charged domestic situation, there were no easy answers. With the wartime housing shortage, tensions within the young household couldn't help but mount. Financial resources were limited to John's salary, which hadn't increased to any meaningful extent throughout the four years of the war.

The lightning rod was the upbringing of John, Jr.— "Johnny" to all those who loved and fiercely protected him. While everyone's heart was in the right place, disagreements abounded over the best way for him to learn and grow. Alice firmly believed that he needed to remain at home where he could learn to do things for himself. John's mother and aunt, both nurses by profession, overprotected the boy and tended to do most things for him. John, as father, found himself in the unusual position of being an outsider, negotiating with the three women who knew Johnny best. He also believed that his son required help and assistance in an institutional setting, which was then the accepted standard for dealing with handicapped children. Alice wouldn't hear of it. She believed and often repeated to her children that there was a place for everyone on God's earth, and Johnny's was with his family. Alice's brother, Eric, would later say, "I think that one of her 'shining moments' was that she stayed by her handicapped son, helping him through life."

In the midst of all this, Alice received word that her

remaining family—mother, two sisters, and brother—had been released from captivity. Edith, her older sister, wrote:

At last we are free—free to breathe again. Three years and eight months buried alive, not knowing what is happening in the world. We feel like "Rip Van Winkle." The world has progressed while we have been asleep. You can imagine what we feel like to be under British rule again. We have all suffered in one way or another. We all know what hunger is...The children used to wake up crying with pains in the tummy. My heart used to bleed to see them suffer and unable to help them. Some people suffered terribly by the hands of Japs. They slapped your face for the least excuse. There have been some severe beatings of internees. We even had some executions and imprisonment. All is over and best forgotten. We are thankful to be alive.

They were free, but homeless and virtually destitute. Emily, Leilah, and Edith and her family were in Hong Kong, and Eric was heading back from a horrific imprisonment in a Japanese POW camp in Osaka—a wrenching experience he would never speak of. When he was released on August 15, 1945, there was nothing left of him but skin and bones. He traveled by train with the other prisoners to the nearest port, where they were taken on board a U.S. Navy hospital ship and given a hot shower, new clothing and a good meal. He spent several months in a resettlement camp before leaving from Manila on the *Admiral Hughes*, an American Navy ship bound for Vancouver Island. Upon arriving, the American POWs were sent on to Seattle, the Canadian POWs were greeted by family and left for home, and Eric and the others in the British Army boarded trains for Nova Scotia. They sailed for England and were discharged there. Eric found work and eventually made the trip to New York, where John met him on the dock and took him home to Alice. Before leaving for Toronto to begin a new life there, he visited John's parents in Millington, New Jersey. After a short recuperation, he departed, to be reunited with his mother and sister.

Once repatriated, Edith and Arthur decided to relocate to Australia, where Arthur's father had been born and where he had many relatives still living. The government required all able-bodied men to stay in Hong Kong to help rebuild the city, so Arthur stayed and put Edith and the children aboard the *Empress of Australia*. But when they arrived in Singapore, Edith once again faced the discrimination of the White Australia Policy when Australian officials told her she could not sail to their country. She and the children were diverted to England instead. Arthur, assuming his family had successfully made the trip, later boarded an aircraft carrier and sailed to Australia, only to discover that Edith was in England. He immediately found passage to England and reconnected with Edith. In England, they joined other refugees at Baginton Fields, a camp that served as a halfway house for refugees, until they could find permanent arrangements in other countries. Emily and Leilah also stayed there for almost a year. When Arthur's family was finally able to make arrangements to sponsor them in Australia in November of 1946, Edith, Arthur, May, and Richard sailed to their new homeland.

Alice worked for several months with her relatives in Canada and corresponded with Emily in England. Emily decided that she and Leilah, together with Eric, would all relocate to Canada with the help of sponsorship for immigration from Cecil's brother, Montagu. Alice was eager to have her family come to North America so they could begin a new life. By 1947, all three would settle in the Toronto area. With financial assistance from Alice and John, Emily, Eric, and Leilah moved into a boarding-house, with shared rooms, a hot plate, and eventually a refrigerator, and began the slow process of rebuilding their lives. Eric found work as a civil engineer. Emily and Leilah sewed for a major department store and Leilah gave piano lessons.

· · · ·

On December 19, 1945, MGM premiered *They Were Expendable* at Loew's Capital Theater in Washington. John and Alice attended what was a glittering, star-studded gala as guests of Fleet Admiral and Mrs. Chester Nimitz. Other guests included actors from the film, Robert Montgomery and Donna Reed, but the most rousing applause was reserved for the true hero of that evening, John Bulkeley. The film was a critical success, and even today is rated highly among the many classic films of director John Ford.

Full of tension, the Bulkeley's marriage began to reflect the feelings John was experiencing personally. With Alice's attention focused on the children—specifically Johnny—John felt overwhelmed by his memories of war and the challenge of trying to fit back into family life. In a way, perhaps, John felt Alice had chosen Johnny's care over him. For her part, Alice had never known John during times of peace. Since the evening they had met on the HMS *Diana*, they had been fighting against a common enemy—the Japanese. She had never seen the more vulnerable side of John as a person who might be in need of comfort. It was hard to comprehend and understand his traumatic and horrific wartime experiences.

One afternoon, as the children played in the next room with Elizabeth, Alice and John argued angrily in the kitchen. That night John packed his bags and told Alice the marriage was over. Although John had been the apple of her eye and only child, Elizabeth stood by Alice's side and, as Joan looked on, closed the door on him.

As the nights turned into weeks, Alice realized John wouldn't be coming back. The war that had taken her father from her physically had now claimed her husband mentally. He was discontented and in a state of despair. She had lost the only man she had ever truly loved. After several months, their divorce was finalized and John, to Alice's surprise, married a New York socialite. Now, Alice felt, John would finally have the "proper" wife who might complement and assist him with his career ambitions in the navy. Although she felt angry and deserted during the months that followed as she struggled to keep her family intact, she knew that John was struggling to find peace within himself and she actually believed that he would come back to her if given the time and space to deal with his inner pain. Alice was aware that John possessed a dual personality. One could be hard and unforgiving, and the other, soft and sentimental. She was hoping against hope that he would return to her someday, but the fighting, the malaria, the dysentery, and other tropical diseases had taken a tremendous toll on him. John had helped to shape larger world events that led to victory in the Pacific, but he had lost his marriage.

Despite his new life, John continued to talk with Alice often about his innermost thoughts and to visit her and the children. As she had always been able to do, she comforted and guided him back from the hellish feelings he had been wrestling with in his mind during the war. He had a malaise of the soul and was searching for meaning in his life. Within a year, he went through another divorce and quickly remarried Alice in their second quiet and very private ceremony.

Aboard the *Stribling*, John typed an intense, searching letter to Alice, dated November 20, 1946, that reveals a remarkable level of introspection from a man so famous for being quick, brisk and duty bound:

> *In regard to religion...the following will be an explanation of my position which holds water anywhere to those who think and to those who desire to understand the way of life. In the final analysis there is only one subject of permanent interest...the soul. The busy average modern man who is rushed on his way by machines, ambition, social and political functions, is apt to discount the importance of spiritual life, if he doesn't overlook its existence. He generally excuses himself for mislaying the wisdom of spiritual values and slips into a life of practical expediency. (me)*

In attempting to align their respective versions of faith, John informs Alice in the letter's concluding paragraph that he is working to lift his own soul to a higher plane, the one where he will need to be to rejoin their lives in the aftermath of everything the young couple—together and separately—has been witness to:

...the pilgrim has felt the presence of God...though he may not yet know the utter joy of walking with God, he apprehends the future of delight that will be his of which signs are revealed daily and hourly...and in a world that has become miraculous.

Family Ties

CHAPTER NINE
1950-1963

Joan, your Mother has made a complete success of her life and
I believe her to have found happiness in her children and in
the small things in life. She has been able to transmit some of
her goodness to me and to all others that have known her.
Therefore, Joan, I counsel you as well as the boys to always
seek counsel and advice from your Mother in times when
temper flares and at times tears flow. Your Mother has the
answer that is as old as time itself. Stay together as a
close-knit family, for in that is your strength.

*Excerpt from the last will and testament of
John Bulkeley written April 6, 1949,
aboard the USS Mt. Olympus*

The Bulkeley family in the 1950s. Clockwise from
upper right: Alice, John Jr., Diana, Joan, Gina and Peter.

For better or for worse, John and Alice had made it through the tremendous trials of a global war and now were faced with focusing on the rest of their lives. They had each discovered an inner strength of character, tested its limits of endurance, and returned to their married life with true confidence in themselves and one another. This prepared them for raising their children, with Alice permanently cast in the role of primary caregiver, and John as the career navy man who re-entered his family's orbit at frequent intervals. It was a mold that many American service families fell into during the post-war years.

The difference with the Bulkeleys was that they chose to mainstream their son Johnny into everyday family life during an era where there was little precedent for raising a child with so many mental and physical handicaps. Alice agreed to an important first step: sending him to a nine-month program at a special school in Delaware where he could be taught how to care for himself. Siblings Joan and Peter quickly developed a strong loyalty to their brother, as it was common for them to defend him against the taunts and sometimes-cruel actions of ignorant playmates. By all accounts, it approached a normal family life, but one that would always hinge on Johnny's special needs.

The family grew larger, too, with the births of Regina

Joy in 1951 and Diana Jean in 1953. With these last two additions, Alice had her hands full, with a vast scope of duties that she attended to. It was further complicated by John's assignment in Korea from October 1952 to March 1954 as commander of Destroyer Division 132. In addition to Johnny's ongoing special needs, she shouldered household management, disciplined the children, volunteered for various community activities (which included founding one of the first Boy Scout troops for handicapped boys), and managed the tight household allowance John provided. At the beginning of each month, she divided his salary between envelopes with categories written on them. If, toward the end of the month, the food allowance was low, the family ate "breakfast" for dinner until the next payday. She had perfected this technique during her years in school, later at Butterfield & Swire and during the rationing war years.

Raising Johnny at home remained one of the most significant challenges not only for Alice, but for all the Bulkeley children as well. Mainstreaming a mentally challenged child was virtually unheard-of in the 1950s. Johnny faced rejection on a daily basis, and, to a large extent, so did his fiercely protective siblings—for having a brother who was "different." Yet as a member of the larger navy family, this conferred a measure of protection that Johnny might not have received had he been in a civilian family.

Throughout the 1950s, John's naval career would hopscotch in a number of different directions, few of which made sense to a man of action, and almost all with the consequence of Alice's uprooting their family to set up housekeeping in a new city and state. With no complaint, she established homes in the navy strongholds of Annapolis, Maryland; Newport, Rhode Island; Washington, D.C.; Norfolk, Virginia; Long Beach, California; and Clarksville, Tennessee.

In Washington, D.C., John was enjoying his assignment with the Atomic Energy Commission, where he was honored to be in the company of Capt. Hyman Rickover, world-class physicists Dr. E. L. Lawrence and J. Robert Oppenheimer, and Dr. Edward Teller, generally credited as the father of the atomic bomb. Though he knew next to nothing about atomic power, he relayed his elation over these impressive new co-workers to Alice, and she smiled and replied, "That's wonderful, dear, but please allow them to express their opinion before telling them where they can go." In September 1952 John was promoted to the rank of captain, his first elevation since the end of World War II.

As is often the case with parents having strongly etched character traits, the Bulkeley children developed distinctive, forceful personalities. Joan, the eldest, sparkled with the poise of a dutiful daughter, having learned early on how to be gracious and effective when caught in the eye of the newsreel cameras. Johnny, with his disabilities and cerebral palsy, appreciated a regular schedule and was ever anxious to do the right things. Peter emerged as the mischievous middle child, in whom Alice must have recognized traces of her own once-merry brother, Eric. Peter was the family adventurer, starting early with an escape from his Queens apartment at the age of two. (Luckily, a police car found him on the sidewalk corner in the dead of winter before he wandered into harm's way.) Gina grew up thoughtful and searching, expressing her belief for a brief time in the civil rights movement of the late 1960s. Diana, the baby of the family, did not follow in the dependent footsteps of a youngest child, and emulated many of her mother's independent traits.

Each child benefited from Alice's tireless efforts. As a young child, Gina suffered from speech problems that affected her self-confidence. Alice made a ritual of practicing drills with her until she conquered the problem. And, as childhood illnesses came and went, each child was lovingly nursed to health by Alice's calm, reassuring hands. These same hands diligently tended a garden that bloomed with azaleas, roses, tulips, and daffodils.

The household environment Alice managed to build was one of great balance between firm discipline and tremendous love, which was shown freely. Although their father was the military man, because he was away so much of the time the children knew Alice was the boss, a nickname she certainly earned from John in her later years. If Alice said, "No," they knew it was the end of the road for their pleas. But they also knew they could turn to Alice with any problem, and so could their friends. She was a genuine sympathizer and an attentive listener. She was also shockproof. They could tell her anything, whether it was about teen romances or other problems. Her advice was honest, and she offered it without criticism. With her words, she always sought to offer comfort and relief and rarely spoke negatively of anyone; instead, she placed people in the best light and encouraged her children to persevere in life, something she had managed to do even during the most challenging times of her life.

Both parents sought to impress upon their children the lessons they had learned in their youth: attending church, assisting with household chores, respecting adults, the importance of manners, curfews, and, especially, completing assignments. At age ten, Peter, without consulting anyone (especially his mother) signed up to be a newsboy with the Long Beach, California, *Press Telegram*. On the first day, he found the stack of newspapers to be delivered stood taller than he was; the second day assumed crisis proportions; and by the third, he had decided to abandon the enterprise. Alice stepped in to teach him the lesson that no one respects a quitter. With the skills of her former secretarial days, she organized his route, started accounting procedures and gave her son's new venture the foundation it needed. She told Peter that he could not quit until he had made a success of the newsboy business. When John returned home after a six-month tour of duty, Alice for once was able to surprise him by waking the weary captain up at 0500 hours the very next morning to assume command of the morning route with Peter. The paper route was "decommissioned" several months later, but only after Peter had made a success of the enterprise.

Peter would again see his mother's determination during his teenage years when, during a heated discussion in their Tennessee military quarters kitchen, he teasingly lifted her up by the waist and set her on the counter. Alice decided her son needed some additional disciplinary training, and with John, began making arrangements for him to attend the New Mexico Military Institute in Roswell, New Mexico, a prep school for military academy-bound young men.

The children discovered new generational ties within an extended family. Their maternal grandmother, uncle, and aunt provided inspiration from not-so-far away

Toronto. But family was lost also. Elizabeth Bulkeley, the independent woman who raised her son alone, Alice's staunchest supporter and beloved "Baba" to her grandchildren, died unexpectedly in New York in 1954 after contracting pneumonia following hip surgery.

In 1956 John was assigned to the Joint Chiefs of Staff in Washington, so the family packed up again and returned to their family home near Silver Spring, Maryland. They were surprised when he was later ordered to be the commanding officer of the USS *Tolovana*, which was homeported in Long Beach. Alice decided not to uproot the family, as John would be away at sea for the majority of time.

Within weeks of deploying to the Far East, and with the *Tolovana* 600 miles from Pearl Harbor, John suffered a hemorrhaging ulcer and had to be transferred under emergency conditions to another ship. He was then flown from Midway Island to the Tripler Medical Center in Honolulu. Alice first received news of this event by telegram. The navy explained it had done everything possible to get him to the nearest hospital but that his condition was grave.

Alice prayed and stayed by the phone for the next four days, realizing that her husband was in critical condition. With five children who depended on her, she was unable to fly to his side. Her prayers were answered when she received the call that the massive transfusion he received at Tripler had saved his life. Following his month-long recovery, John packed gifts for everyone in the family and returned home to celebrate. But this medical incident would nearly cost John his career.

The brass' subsequent assignment made him despair.

Even though he was America's most decorated warrior, he was given orders to report to the Clarksville Naval Base, a defense atomic support agency in Tennessee. The naval base was referred to as "the bird cage," mostly because of its electrically charged fences—which protected the navy command deep within Fort Campbell, Kentucky, home of the 101st Airborne Division. This was about as far from the ocean as a sailor could get. Alice recalled it as a time of crisis:

> *I had never seen John so disheartened. He even toyed with the idea of resigning from the navy he had always loved so dearly. John was convinced that the navy brass were putting him on a back burner, that at age forty-eight he was being sidetracked to a job as a paper shuffler and had reached a dead end in his career. The admiral's stars he had coveted since boyhood now seemed to be fading away.*

After two weeks of reflecting, John reported to the Clarksville Naval Base with Alice and the children following him there. Joan was away at this time studying at the University of Maryland. John immediately improved the base security and raised morale. Alice volunteered for service organizations such as the American Red Cross and was looked up to by all the base wives. The family's fortunes were about to change, however, as John Fitzgerald Kennedy, the young man who John had endorsed for PT boat service in Chicago in 1942, was sworn in as president of the United States in January 1961.

Showdown at Guantanamo

CHAPTER TEN
1963-1966

Does this mean we won't have tea this afternoon?

*Alice Wood Bulkeley after hearing that the
pipe supplying water from Cuba to
the Guantanamo Naval Base was cut.*

John and Alice (pictured in 1964) participated in many base
ceremonies, which helped build morale among the military families.

A newly promoted Rear Admiral Bulkeley took command of the U.S. Naval Base at Guantanamo Bay, Cuba, in December 1963, one of the cold war's major flash points. The devastating assassination of President Kennedy a month before had shocked America to its core. Alice, Johnny, Gina, and Diana accompanied him to New York for the trip to "Gitmo." Boarding the *Geiger*, the ship that would take them there, Alice tightly clutched the same small handkerchief she once held while leaving China, as she shepherded her children into their cabin with Clover, the family's Siamese cat. John headed for the bridge.

Only months before, John received a telegram from JFK that announced the commander-in-chief's intention to promote him to rear admiral, a promotion that would be the fulfillment of a lifelong aspiration. It had read, in part: "I was delighted that your name was on the list [of recommended candidates]. I am sure that this is a richly deserved promotion and I offer you my congratulations." The telegram had arrived while Alice, John, and Joan were visiting the Defense Atomic Agency Field Command Headquarters at Sandia, New Mexico. They were out for the afternoon, but upon returning, discovered that two admiral's stars had been placed on the door of John's personal quarters. Alice recalled that upon entering the

room, the phone rang and it was President Kennedy himself. More phone calls followed, with people stopping by
to congratulate the admiral. Dinner that evening was a ju-
bilant celebration. This promotion led to another formal
invitation to the White House—this time under far more
triumphant circumstances than when Captain Bulkeley had
met there with JFK while on his Clarksville assignment.

Here, at last, was the prize that this heroic sailor of the
old navy had pursued since the age of twelve—the coveted
two stars that Alice had always feared would be denied to
her husband in part because of her Eurasian background.
And yet, on the eve of their silver wedding anniversary
(November 10, 1963), the couple was able to recollect
how John had been told within a week of his marriage to
Alice that he had made a terrible mistake in taking her as
his wife, and that his naval career was in jeopardy.

"I realized the terrible dilemma my husband was going through, for he loved the Navy. It was his whole life,
and I knew he had a great future and would some day
become Admiral," Alice wrote later of those very early
days of her married life.

Now, twenty-five years later, they embarked on the
admiral's most challenging command: defending what *Life*
magazine had headlined as "The United States' Most Vulnerable Fortress." Located on the southern shore of Cuba,
Guantanamo Bay is a thirty-one square-mile area that has
been under U.S. control since 1898, when U.S. Marines
stormed ashore during the Spanish-American War and
helped the colony of Cuba gain its independence. In 1903,
the Cuban government signed the Guantanamo Treaty,
granting the United States permanent jurisdiction and con-

trol over the area. After Fidel Castro seized power in 1959, the dictator promptly sought the expulsion of the American military using every possible stratagem. In outlining the new admiral's duties to him, Attorney General Robert F. Kennedy had been blunt: "Show that bastard with the beard who's boss in this part of the world." John Bulkeley's mission was clear: defend the key United States naval base, stand up to Castro's threats, but most importantly, avoid igniting World War III.

And that was precisely where the world was sitting in late 1963: astride a powder keg that could once again ignite a global conflict and nuclear annihilation. A tough, unpredictable new admiral was at the helm, and one wrong decision on his part could have disastrous consequences.

For Alice, there were strong parallels between her husband's latest posting and her early years. Like the Swatow of her youth, Guantanamo was a sheltered deep-water harbor, situated in a tropical climate, with U.S. warships on patrol, offering vestiges of the colonial lifestyle she had known. And like the bombarded port she had known in the years after college and prior to her marriage, Guantanamo was seething with high tempers, intrigue, and treachery as two world powers squared off, with her family once again planted squarely in the middle.

For John, there was scarcely time to catch his breath amid an onslaught of threats and underhanded tactics launched by "the Maximum Leader," the title Castro had adopted. Once again, as ever, the odds seemed overwhelmingly stacked against the fifty-three year-old American admiral. Cuba had an army of 250,000 Soviet-trained soldiers, backed by Soviet-built tanks, aircraft, missiles, and other modern weaponry. The admiral had approximately 1,000 men in the 1st Batallion, Sixth Marines, a squadron of jets, some armed helicopters, a limited number of tanks, and U.S. warships anchored in the bay. They were surrounded on three sides by hostile forces, their backs to the sea. John responded to this challenge by erecting an enormous Marine emblem and illuminating it for the Cuban soldiers to see. (It was repainted when the admiral died and remains at Gitmo today.)

Yet an oasis of family life managed to prevail in the hothouse atmosphere and, as tensions mounted, Alice and John kept their children feeling secure by displaying a great sense of humor. Instead of dwelling on John's new life as a literal target—even escalating to the point of an assassination attempt—they simply laughed about their circumstances when around the children to divert their attention away from the serious situation.

As was her custom whenever the Bulkeleys moved, Alice set to work immediately to transform their quarters. Bags and trunks were quickly unpacked. The family Siamese cat checked out the new quarters, adding an immediate familiarity, and Alice's implacable custom of 4 P.M. teatime anchored each day.

The admiral's residence on Deer Point was a tranquil sanctuary with royal palm trees at the end of a long driveway. The vast villa, with its colonial plantation façade and sweeping verandas resembled her former Swatow home. Surrounded by fragrant, night-blooming jasmine and cereus, it overlooked the aquamarine waters of the bay and its fine, amber-colored sand beaches.

Joan had married and settled in Illinois in December 1962, and Pete was attending the New Mexico Military

Institute and would soon be sworn in at the Naval Academy in Annapolis. Only three children—Johnny, Gina, and Diana—rounded out the Bulkeley family presence. Alice's role as the wife of an admiral carried additional responsibilities, including serving as a role model to the other military wives and families on the base. She was responsible for setting the standard for social life, which involved planning key observances, welcoming and hosting visiting dignitaries, and participating in or leading service organizations. Guests were frequent and included Bob Hope and his troupe for a Christmas show, Cardinal Francis Spellman, senators, members of Congress, and the news media.

Vice Admiral Gerald Miller recalled of Alice and John during that time:

> *She was a beautiful woman with a sharp mind, and could recount experiences in her life that were not the norm for many navy wives...It was obvious that like so many service wives of that period in history, she had lived in the shadow of a colorful hero of our country. It was also obvious that he adored her immensely...There was a gleam in his eye and almost a smile on his face as his pride in Alice Wood Bulkeley shone through.*

To help manage all this, for the first time in more than two decades, Alice actually had household help, in the form of six navy stewards. Dinner was served formally with the stewards in attendance, just as when Alice was a child and changed into one of her flouncy dresses with a pinafore for dinner in the British tradition to which her father adhered. These men came to appreciate and admire Alice, and did their best to please her. The Bulkeley children, particularly Gina and Diana, quickly came to know that the stewards, who cooked, cleaned, and answered phones, could also facilitate their chores. Alice just as promptly set the girls straight: the stewards were there as a result of their father's rank, which he had earned and they had not. So the girls were still assigned their chores.

Instead of being a remote figure to his family away at sea, John now was able to spend more time with Alice. In some ways, it seemed like a second honeymoon during the three years that John was assigned to Guantanamo. (In fact, they were able to have a romantic holiday away from Gitmo only once during this time—a trip to St. Thomas and St. Croix in 1965.) Despite the relentless tensions, here at last was an opportunity to recapture some of the early romance against a Caribbean backdrop. To assist in this, John brought along his favorite toy forged during the frustrations of his assignment in Tennessee: a sailboat that he personally had constructed from scratch. It was a twenty-six-foot sloop that he christened *Drumbeat.* Alice and John sailed together across Guantanamo Bay, but the boat was used for more than idyllic tours. Amelia Fales, an officer's wife, pointed out:

> *Admiral Bulkeley had built his personal sailboat himself and on the few occasions when he had free time he puttered around with it or sailed it on Guantanamo Bay. There were times when the Admiral asked my husband [navy captain] Bill and I to go sailing with him. Bill always enjoyed this, but I*

became wary about going along. Every jaunt was an adventure. Admiral Bulkeley would chase Russian cargo ships, then sail out to see if vessels guarding the bay entrance were alert. I had visions of someone blasting us out of the water, so I started coming up with excuses not to go.

Joan also remembered a late afternoon sail with her father during one of her visits to Guantanamo, and her alarm when they sailed across the bow of an inbound aircraft carrier. "I looked at this enormous ship bearing down on us but Dad didn't seem at all worried." The admiral's only comment to her was: "No need to worry. We're under sail so we have the right of way."

John's calm, protective nature extended to all of his children. While snorkeling with Diana off a reef at Blue Beach (the only beach in Gitmo without rocks ringing it to keep the sharks out) he spotted a six-foot blue shark about six feet away. John slowly turned Diana away and gently pushed her back toward shore, keeping his body between her and the shark. "I wasn't scared at all," Diana recalled, "because he was with me."

Alice is quick to puncture attempts to overly romanticize day-to-day (and night) life on the base, especially given the extreme seriousness of her husband's responsibilities:

John had always kidded me about sleeping like a log. So I didn't even wake up when he climbed into bed with me at about 3:30 on this morning, after he had been on the go for 24 hours. After tramping for miles along the fence line, John was so exhausted that he hadn't even removed his uniform or muddy com-

bat boots. The first clue I had that he had been in bed was when I was awakened shortly after dawn and saw mud from his boots on the sheet. By then, he had already left for headquarters, having slept less than two hours.

Later he joked that I shouldn't sleep so soundly, that it might have been some Marine climbing in bed with me.

While the events of those days have been extensively documented in numerous books and countless newspaper and media reports, it's still difficult to recapture the paranoia and realistic worldwide fear that one misstep could escalate and result in nuclear holocaust. Castro zeroed in on Guantanamo and mounted a howling propaganda campaign to drive the "Yankee imperialists" from the island. After John Kennedy's assassination, Castro directed his vitriol towards Kennedy's last emissary—the square-jawed Admiral Bulkeley. And so began a three-year duel of brinkmanship, with Bulkeley mastering every trick that Castro and his army could muster.

This culminated in a battle over the naval base's water supply, which Castro threatened to cut off (and eventually did), as it was supplied by Cuba. The base had to check the safety of the water hourly. Castro had been accusing the base of stealing water, and the admiral responded to this accusation by ordering the water supply pipeline to be severed in full view of the press. Then, with the entire world as witness, Castro accused the admiral of continuing to steal Cuba's water. In a fury, and in full view of the Cuban army and a contingent of reporters, the admiral ordered the water pipe supplying the base to be dug up and cut open, and showed the world that the pipe was bone dry. It was a masterstroke. Castro was exposed as a liar. America cheered its fast-acting hero. "Admiral Bulkeley hit 'em where it hurts. He made Castro eat his lie, without any water to wash it down," declared the *Miami Herald.* Admiral Bulkeley then launched plans to have a desalination plant installed as fast as possible on the base. Until it was built, water would have to be brought in from Florida. Alice was heard asking, "Does this mean we won't have tea this afternoon?"

On July 30, 1964, Alice, wearing a beige linen dress and matching hat, was the center of attention at a ceremony as she turned on the water from the new desalination plant. With the admiral and many of the base personnel and news media in attendance, she turned the ship's wheel and the water flowed. John then placed at the site a new sign for Cuba that read, "U.S. Answer to Castro—Gitmo Water Liberated from Cuba at this point."

Following this resounding triumph, the entire base breathlessly awaited Castro's next move. Bulkeley was astonished to discover that the latest rumor sweeping over the base was that all hell was about to break loose and that he had evacuated his entire family to the United States during the night. He promptly went to the base's television station to stomp out the demoralizing rumors. "'My family is at home, and they will stay put," he emphasized, in his famous staccato voice. "There will be no official evacuation—repeat, no evacuation—of dependents and civil service employees." However, he added, "anyone who wants to leave...will be furnished transportation back to the States." Alice and John then made public appearances on the base to reassure the personnel and their families.

Although two hundred civil service employees duly packed and left for the States, not a single military family departed. Adversity had brought out the best in them. "God, I'm proud of our ladies!" Bulkeley boasted to his staff about the military wives. Some of those remarks, no doubt, centered on Alice, who worked tirelessly in as many ways as she could to build morale and lift everyone's spirits. For in spite of the tropical climate, the picturesque views of the azure Caribbean, and the Sierra Madre range rising up sharply behind the shoreline, the naval base was effectively cut off from the rest of the world. "Island fever" was palpable, and only magnified with each new incident in the war of nerves. Rumors flew about the base at roughly the speed of light. As Natalie Lindon, the wife of the admiral's chief of staff, recalled:

> *Navy wives, especially those of us at Gitmo during this crisis period, were a close-knit family, but it was hard to overcome the feeling of isolation. It was necessary to keep busy, but periodic defense exercises on the base kept us reminded of our constant vulnerability.*

In late August 1964 the families of Gitmo fell victim to another foe, Mother Nature, when hurricane Cleo pounded the island. For several days the storm, which was considered an unusually wet storm, whipped the island with rain and wind. The palm trees at Deer Point bent to the ground as the Bulkeley children huddled inside the house. Johnny was terrified and Alice worked to soothe his nerves and those of the other children by talking about the typhoon she had survived in Swatow as a young girl. When it was no longer safe to stay in the house, Alice took the family to the officers' club, where they spent the night. Following the storm, Alice and the other military wives had the task of cleaning up. The base school was flooded and took two full weeks to restore to normal. Upon her return, Gina noticed the stains on the walls of her classroom where the water had left its mark.

In the eye of the storm that constantly swirled around them at Gitmo stood the calm determination of Alice, despite days when her daughters awoke to the sounds of windows rattling from gunfire. She volunteered as a "pink lady" at the base hospital. She founded a Girl Scout troop, benefiting both her daughters. As there were no special education facilities on Guantanamo to accommodate Johnny's needs, Alice set about interesting him in ceramics classes and continuing his piano instruction. She participated in sports events, concerts, dances, and hosted formal luncheons and dinners—emulating the style of her late father, Captain Wood. With her family tended to, she then applied every tactic she could think of to help the base's civilian population of 2,500 pass the grinding hours.

Alice and John's Christmas parties also echoed the traditions her late father had established so many years before at his club in Swatow. The main difference was that the hosts often left these holiday parties to wish the Marines on fencerow duty a Merry Christmas and to deliver holiday treats that young Gina and Diana had baked for them. John even treated the Cuban soldiers to his version of an appropriate Christmas greeting in 1964. He arranged for the placement of a giant sign facing the enemy to be lit by floodlights. The Marines were delighted by its subtle jab at the Cubans: "Peace on Earth to Men of Good Will."

These impromptu visits by "Big Iron" and his lady were the highlight of the day for the Marines. Alice's feminine appearance and warm smile cheered them. When they stopped for a brief time, the Marines were even more alert and protective of them.

The Bulkeleys' generosity extended beyond their small community on the base. On April 8, 1966, around midnight, John received word that an SOS had been sent from the *Viking Princess*, a cruise ship with more than 600 passengers and crew aboard sailing from Aruba to Miami, which had experienced an explosion at sea. The admiral immediately sent several jets to find the distressed vessel and report back. Once the ship was located, he dispatched all available navy vessels to the scene. As the rescued passengers arrived at the base, wet and badly shaken, they were greeted by John, Alice, three chaplains, and numerous military wives who were ready to comfort them. In a spectacular rescue, John's men succeeded in saving every last person. Two elderly passengers died of heart attacks while in the lifeboats. Before leaving for the States, several passengers stopped by the Bulkeleys' house to thank Alice for her kindness during their ordeal.

The admiral commanded the respect of all his men and though he demanded much, he also walked the lines and kept the same vigils. The same respect was accorded Alice, who kept up a demanding schedule while raising a family. The couple was ever-present in the daily affairs of the base and their hard work and sacrifice won them many admirers, including Marine Colonel Anthony Walker:

All of us Marines at Gitmo felt an affection for Admiral Bulkeley. On his birthday [August 19], at

*oh-six-hundred [6 a.m.], some 400 of us Marines
jogged to his quarters on Deer Point and gave three
cheers for the Bulkeleys. The Admiral and his family came out in various sorts of dress, and we presented him with a present, suitably engraved, a me-
mento of our serving with him. Then we jogged off
to the hills. This sort of thing pleased Bulkeley, I
believe, but most admirals would have blanched.*

Enjoying the moment, Alice stood on the balcony in
her flowered silk kimono, beaming and waving at the rug-
ged young men.

$\mathcal{H}$ail and $\mathcal{F}$arewell

CHAPTER ELEVEN
1967-1996

I am looking forward to seeing you awfully, awfully much. And I have been terribly lonely without you—almost unbearable.
Love always and always.

Letter to Alice from John

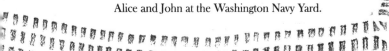

Alice and John at the Washington Navy Yard.

After more than three years at Guantanamo, Alice was finally able to pack up her family for their next move to Norfolk, Virginia, for John's next assignment at sea with the Sixth Atlantic Fleet. It was not without regret that they made their farewells in Cuba; it had been an around-the-clock challenge for John at Gitmo, but with so much to do and his family all together, the time had flown by. After a brief tour in Norfolk, the admiral and his wife would return once more to Washington, D.C., at the Washington Navy Yard in "Quarters D." This would be home for the next twenty-two years, and the significance of their tenure at this address would eventually result in these quarters being renamed in the admiral's honor. Gina and Diana would go off to Penn Hall in Pennsylvania, and Johnny would remain at home and become the organist for the Navy Yard Chapel, playing for the Protestant service often attended by presidents and visiting dignitaries.

For the first time in the Bulkeley family history, a black cat would move in and take over the house. Peter had found "Blackie" in a sewer and rescued him. He was malnourished and his fur was matted, but he showed a feisty spirit. John took to him right away and instructed

Alice to buy the best tins of select tuna for him. At the sound of a can opening, Blackie, like lightning, would streak through the kitchen door.

"Quarters D" was a historical four-story colonial home with a front and back staircase. With fireplaces in each sitting room, it was a comfortable home filled to the brim with Alice and John's mementoes and collections. Two stewards kept the house in order and Alice let everyone know that she was indeed "the boss," the pet name John still affectionately used.

In the meantime, John had accepted the command of the Naval Board of Inspection and Survey, better known as Insurv. The admiral was now responsible for making certain that the navy was ready for combat action at any time. He was directly responsible to the Chief of Naval Operations and the Secretary of the Navy for the readiness conditions of all navy surface ships, aircraft, submarines, and weapons systems. It was an intense undertaking, and over more than two decades, he logged more than 2.5 million air miles in addition to another 500,000 on the ground. His blistering, demanding reports on substandard equipment and operations would raise political hackles within the navy and all across the nation's capital.

He quickly became notorious for his particular application of the phrase, "Just thought you'd like to know." The admiral was disturbed when other admirals claimed ignorance of a situation after John had pushed to have a serious ship deficiency corrected. So he ordered his staff to draw up a catalog-sized mailing list and, following each inspection by Insurv, he wrote a candid letter detailing deficiencies and sent it directly to the appropriate admiral. Each letter concluded with "Just thought you'd like to know," and was copied and sent to his vast distribution list.

Referring to John's Insurv position, Rear Adm. William R. Schmidt, USN, president of Inspection and Survey recalled that, "no name in the 132-year history of Insurv is more revered than Admiral Bulkeley...a true naval legend. His motivation and driving force as president was the well-being and the safety of our sailors, as well as ensuring that our ships were ready for sustained combat at any time."

As he set to cleaning house with his customary bravado, Alice quietly and efficiently reestablished the Bulkeley home headquarters in Washington. But the household itself was changing. The Bulkeley children had all reached adulthood and left the family nest. With more time to devote to projects outside the family, Alice and John took on a personal project with special meaning for them: the restoration of the Navy Yard Chapel, an old building on the grounds that had fallen into disrepair. Experiencing Alice's generosity and hard work firsthand, Chaplain (Capt.) Bill Perry said of her in 1991:

> *Alice is a living saint. She would never agree to that assessment, but then, saints never do. However, to meet her is to know intuitively that you are in the presence of someone special. If you want to meet a genuine living saint, I offer you the choice of traveling to India to shake hands with Mother Teresa or simply coming to the Washington Navy Yard Chapel for this Sunday's Protestant worship service and meeting Alice Bulkeley.*

The admiral and his "laughing lady" as he sometimes

called her attended Washington functions throughout the Johnson, Nixon, Ford, Carter, and Reagan administrations. During an inaugural ball for President Carter, Alice was kissed on the cheek by the new president, after which First Lady Rosalyn Carter was heard to ask him why he had made the surprising gesture. President Carter simply replied that he wanted to thank her for the travails that she had endured as the wife of a Medal of Honor recipient. Alice managed a warm smile at each gala when John would inevitably remind her: "You're a long way from Kialat Road." Indeed she was.

From time to time, that long road produced cherished visitors. In 1968 Joan arranged a sentimental surprise for Alice in Chicago: a reunion with her sister Edith, whom Alice hadn't seen in nearly thirty years. Tears, smiles and gales of laughter followed, before everyone flew on to Toronto for a truly joyous Christmas reunion with brother Eric, sister Leilah, and mother Emily. It was an especially poignant moment for Emily Wood to have her children all around her once more. (She lived on in good health and was baptized at the age of seventy before passing away, at home, at the age of ninety-four.)

During the admiral's tenure at Insurv, the Bulkeleys traveled frequently, including annual trips to England to visit Beaumaris, the Bulkeley family's ancestral home, and to France and the beaches of Normandy. At the American cemetery and at other cemeteries, Alice would place roses on the gravesites for the lost lives of many nations, including Germany. She worked tirelessly on behalf of the Navy Yard Chapel and was active in Navy Relief.

As is often the case with lives well-lived, both John and Alice were able to revisit places of their youth during their later years. In 1977 the admiral returned to the Philippines and Corregidor. It was a highly emotional experience for the old sailor, the former "Wild Man of the Philippines," to revisit the north dock and recollect the vivid memories of the breakout and escape through the enemy blockade and mined waters, when he departed on *PT-41* with General MacArthur, his family, and select members of his staff. He and Alice were overwhelmed with attention and affection from the Filipino people and surrounded by photographers and reporters.

Tragedy struck the Bulkeley family in the fall of 1981, testing the faith of all three generations. Peter Tare Bulkeley, the firstborn child to Carol and Peter Bulkeley, was already a shining light among Alice and John's grandchildren at the age of two-and-a-half years old. The entire family simply called him by his middle name, Tare. With his white-blond hair, Tare already bore a stunning resemblance to his father as a young boy and had his mother's smile. In San Diego on September 8, while briefly in the care of a trusted babysitter, the toddler fell into a pool at the babysitter's home and was not found for nearly an hour due to a pool cover that prevented him from being seen. During the agonizing wait at the hospital, Carol phoned Alice.

"Please ask God for His help because you are closer to him than I am," Carol said. Alice gently told her that God loves us all, but that she would pray for Tare.

The little boy never regained consciousness and died three days later in the hospital, cradled by his mother and by his father, who had been at sea and was flown back on emergency leave by the navy. Alice and John flew immediately to California to be at Carol's side, followed by other members of the family, during the heartbreaking vigil. Although shaken, Alice focused on supporting Carol, who had just given birth to a baby girl, Lauren, only two weeks before the tragedy. With Tare's death, Carol, who had always kept a diary, found it too painful to write and re-read what she had written. She quit her lifelong habit, just as Alice had done nearly forty years earlier, days after Johnny's birth. Little Peter Tare was buried at Arlington National Cemetery.

In late 1984, accompanied by Joan, Alice made a pilgrimage of her own to Hong Kong for the fiftieth reunion of her Hong Kong University class. It was a heartening experience for her to know that the two educational institutions she had known there—the Diocesan Girls' School on Kowloon and HKU—had grown and prospered through the years, and to see for herself how Hong Kong had remained a vibrant and glittering port with modern ships contrasting with the traditional junks and sampans. However, Hong Kong had swelled from a population of 300,000 to more than 6 million residents.

It was a time of reflection and many memories for this woman and her abiding faith, as she reserved time to visit the graves of a number of friends who had died defending Hong Kong from Japanese invaders, including Donald Anderson. She and Joan made a special visit to his grave accompanied by Donald's sister, who now served as the headmistress of the DGS. Another stop was made at the Stanley Market (now famous for its bargain shopping) adjacent to Stanley Prison, where her family had been imprisoned during the war. Alice had wanted to see the area for herself and to visit the camp cemetery for a few moments of quiet remembrance of those terrifying years.

Although Swatow, renamed Shantou, was only 175 miles to the northwest of Hong Kong, she chose to leave it untouched by modern memories.

On January 31, 1988, John and Alice flew from wintry Washington, D.C., to balmy Guantanamo for a ceremony to name a new building, "Bulkeley Hall." When the admiral cut the ribbon opening the new facility alongside Rear Admiral Thomas Emery, Commander, Training Command, U.S. Atlantic Fleet, it marked one of the few times in naval history that a ship or building had been named for a living hero.

Alice and John enjoyed and looked forward to participating in the annual reunions of PT Boats, Inc. and the USS *Endicott,* DD495, held in different parts of the country. Although PT boatmen scattered to the four corners over the course of World War II, they reunited in this context. Another organization, the Peter Tares, was formed in 1947 at the New York Yacht Club, where John (and later Peter) was a member. The Bulkeleys became fast friends with the founder of PT Boats, Inc., James M. "Boats" Newberry, who began a one-page Christmas letter to former PT comrades in 1946, and lived to see it become a forty-eight-page semiannual newspaper before his death in 1985. The annual reunions that Boats organized so well became the highlight of the year for the PT boaters who came with their sea stories. The admiral was often the guest speaker and Alice and Boats' wife, Alyce, became good friends. "From the moment I met her, I loved her," she said of Alice. Today, Alyce Newberry and her daughter carry on the tradition.

As commemorations of World War II events multiplied, so did the occasions for the admiral to cross paths with people he had known before they, too, had moved up in their careers. One such opportunity occurred in 1984, when he met up again with someone he had known as a witty English lieutenant and occasional drinking companion. He, too, had been elevated to the status of admiral—but by virtue of his marriage to the Queen of England. As ever, John was unimpressed with lofty titles like "Duke of Edinburgh," so when he stepped up to greet Prince Philip at a reception in the royal couple's honor in San Diego, he simply fired off a direct and amusing question: "In World War II you and I were both navy lieutenants, we both married Englishwomen, and now you are a five-star admiral and the best I could do was two stars. Where did I go wrong?"

The prince grinned and fired back. "You married the wrong Englishwoman," he said. Although John didn't say so at the time, and with all due respect to Elizabeth II, he disagreed.

In 1988, after fifty-eight years of service to his country, John Bulkeley received his last promotion to the rank of vice admiral and his third star. In a quiet ceremony held in the office of the Chief of Naval Operations (CNO) at the Pentagon with Joan and Peter present, John turned to Alice and proudly pinned a brooch of three stars with diamonds on his "First Mate" of nearly fifty years. CNO Admiral Trost then granted his only request of his navy and his country at the end of his active career. The admiral's flag lieutenant simply opened the office door and the new vice admiral, accompanied by Alice, walked through, their active life in the navy closed forever.

In the summer of 1994, Helen Copley became friendly with the Bulkeleys while researching a book on the life of one of the Bulkeleys' friends, renowned artist and illustrator Howard Chandler Christy, who painted John from life in New York after World War II. That life-sized portrait today resides at the Naval Academy in Annapolis. In *The Christy Quest*, Copley remembers the Bulkeleys welcoming her into their home filled with a lifetime of mementoes:

> *...the Stars and Stripes waved us into the Bulkeleys' Silver Spring driveway. We had just parked our car when the Admiral emerged from his front door. Behind him came Alice, petite and almost hidden behind her khaki-uniformed husband. I threw down the heavy bag I was carrying and ran up the sidewalk to hug them both. It was a wonderful moment. John Bulkeley fit my mental image of what a retired naval hero would look like: strong and sure, gruff but kind and with an adventurous gleam in his eyes. H. Alice was dear, as pretty as a little bird and with a slight British accent which complemented her soft words.*

After a memorable day, Copley left with the same memory that all the Bulkeley children and grandchildren have of saying good-bye to them: "As we pulled away, I looked back. The American flag moved gently above the Bulkeleys who stood together, arms entwined."

And as they always did, John and Alice would remain until the departing guests were completely out of sight.

This lovely twilight of their retirement years was filled with appearances at World War II commemorations, which culminated in Admiral Bulkeley's proud role in the fortieth anniversary of D-Day with President and Mrs.

Reagan, and the fiftieth with Joan, Peter and their spouses attending the first memorial service on board the USS *Washington,* with President and Mrs. Clinton. Later in 1995, on Veteran's Day, a bronze bust of Admiral John Bulkeley was unveiled by Alice, Joan, Gina, and Diana at the Naval Academy in Annapolis. Ann La Rose, the sculptor, and her husband, Bruce, were present with many Bulkeleys and their friends. The bronze bust took center stage and Alice and John were happy to share it. Over the years, additional bronze busts have been placed in the Naval War College at Newport, Rhode Island, and the Naval Amphibious Base at Coronado, California, where a building had been named in the admiral's honor on May 6, 1994. This is the home of Naval Special Boat Squadron One, attached to the Navy's Elite Naval Special Warfare (SEALS).

One month later, in December 1995, the eighty-four-year-old John bravely faced a diagnosis of congestive heart failure and accepted this challenge to die at home with his daughter Gina as his private nurse. Diana comforted him by planting some of his favorite annuals in the garden in the early spring. Peter and Joan took care of the necessary planning and arrangements, readying the family for the tributes that would follow his passing. His last days at home were filled with visits from all his children and their spouses and every grandchild. He died peacefully without ever a complaint—stoic to the end, with Alice holding his hand and whispering endearments. A week before his death, John had told Gina that he would die that night. He hugged and kissed Alice after giving her a Medal of Honor rosette, as he felt that she had performed beyond the call of duty as his wife and mother of their children.

Alice herself did not believe that the life of her husband was indeed ebbing away until almost the very end. But as endings go, it was a fine finish: the old sailor passed away with dignity, surrounded by his family, on April 6, 1996. The flowers Diana had planted died a few days later, succumbing to a spring frost.

The night before John's funeral, his family gathered in a boardroom at the Ritz Carlton Pentagon City hotel for a small family dinner. Alice's children presented her with a gold anchor mounted on a cross, a gift that Alice said at the time represented her strong faith and her love for the navy. She wears the gift, suspended from a gold chain, every day.

The following day, in a moving tribute at Arlington National Cemetery, several speakers including Peter recounted John's life as family, friends, and numerous Washington dignitaries looked on. Adm. Jeremy M. Boorda, Chief of Naval Operations, captured the essence of the moment in his remarks:

Will Rogers said that "We can't all be heroes. Some of us have to stand on the curb and clap as they go by." We gather here today in this place meant for heroes and applaud as a true American Hero passes by...and as we come together here, the rest of America cheers for a man who symbolizes the very best about our Navy and our nation. I have saved the best part—the most important part—John was so blessed to have a tremendous family that loved him and stood by him every step of the way. He was serving in China in 1937 when he met an enchanting English girl and his life and hers would never be the same. That day marked the beginning of an exciting adventure that would last for almost 60 years: an adventure full of laughter and tears, joy and sadness, good times and tough times, but most of all an adventure full of love—love for each other and love for life.

When asked to reflect on his life just before he died, John responded that life had passed too quickly but that his service in the navy had been useful to his country. With full honors, he was buried just down the hill from another PT boat veteran—President John F. Kennedy. His daughter, Diana, recalled the atmosphere surrounding the ceremony:

> *Howitzers started booming as we left the chapel and ended when we reached the gravesite. Twenty-one volleys went off, and I heard bells tolling and the clinking of officers' medals. As I looked around the cemetery, the apple tree blossoms were falling and I thought how beautiful this was for Dad.*

As the graveside service came to a close, Alice approached John's grave and placed a loving tribute of their years together—a bouquet of bright yellow roses.

Return to the Sea

CHAPTER TWELVE
1996-2001

Eternal Father, Strong to save,
Whose arm hath bound the restless wave,
Who bid'st the mighty Ocean deep
Its own appointed limits keep;
O hear us when we cry to thee,
for those in peril on the sea.

The Navy Hymn

The USS *Bulkeley* (DDG-84) is an Aegis Guided
Missile Destroyer homebased in Norfolk, Virginia.

In her living room, Alice carefully raised the glass lid from the wooden case and gently picked up her remaining handkerchief. Her delicate fingertips brushed over the intricate patterns of embroidered arabesques and scalloped roses. Over many years, the other handkerchiefs had been given away, one by one, handed down by her as cherished gifts to her daughters, granddaughters and a great-granddaughter. Surrounded by a collage of framed photographs and mementoes including a replica of her father's barograph, she smiled as she looked about her cozy setting, as the pastel hues of the morning sun streamed into the room. Suddenly, her hazel eyes sparkled and she carefully folded the handkerchief into her purse—the one that matched her new navy blue knit suit. Once more, she would leave to greet a ship.

In June 2000, she traveled to Pascagoula, Mississippi, for the christening of a newly built, Aegis-guided missile destroyer to be named the USS *Bulkeley*. Family, friends and former shipmates came to honor the late Admiral Bulkeley, and to be a part of the traditional christening ceremony that reaches back into the dim recesses of recorded history. On June 24, the christening took place at the Litton Ingalls shipyard with dignitaries, navy admirals and the U. S. Navy Band. Alice was pleased that her daughters Joan, Gina, and Diana, and her daughter-in-law, Carol, were asked by the Secretary of Navy to be the family sponsors. Alice was delighted to be Matron of Honor. Navy representatives included Sarah Fargo, the wife of Adm. Thomas Fargo, USN, and Commander in Chief of the U.S. Pacific Fleet, and Carla Fargo, her sister-in-law. Wearing her hat with her own three stars, Alice kissed the ship and smiled—even though she was confined to a wheelchair for the first time in her life due to a fall. It stirred her to hear the words of another war hero, Senator Robert Dole, who said at the christening: "I don't believe there can be a better inspiration for a warship than that of Vice Admiral Bulkeley. He was a courageous warrior. He was an inspirational leader. He was a fine human being."

Each of the sponsors gave their own tributes in words and salutes, with Joan summing up her family's feelings to the crowd:

> *All of us here know Dad's story—a remarkable one of faith and courage in a difficult period of our nation's history. His spirit and devotion to our navy will be an inspiration and a challenge to all who sail on board the USS Bulkeley. My sincere thank you to all the distinguished guests, our Navy, Litton Ingalls Shipbuilding and to friends and shipmates of Dad's who came here today honoring a man who never sought to be a hero. But, when his country called, he did his duty and more. On behalf of my mother and our entire family, thank you for this magnificent tribute. May this ship sail in a world at peace and may God bless those who sail with her.*

Determined not to use the wheelchair any longer than necessary, Alice promptly "graduated" to a designer cane with inlaid flower petals. She pushed herself to recover and on December 8, 2001, she participated in the commissioning ceremony of the USS *Bulkeley* (DDG-84). Once again, she found herself in the embrace of an ever-growing family, dear friends, and the navy that both she and John so loved. On that day, Comdr. Carlos Del Toro proudly took command of the *Bulkeley* crew, who worked tirelessly preparing the ship for this traditional ceremony. And with his bronze bust in its place of honor on the main deck, the stern gaze of the admiral once again looks out over the ever-changing seas.

Although Alice has crossed oceans and continents, with the world often crossing swords in her wake, she still regards her life as a simple journey. At first glance, this seems incredulous. She found the love of her life, a man who hailed from the twentieth century's most powerful nation, then made it to refuge in the United States, and remained true to her core values as she raised a large family over the course of a long life. She also became part of the navy family, which is steeped in tradition and the calling to serve one's country. Alice respected this and embodied the model navy wife, giving John her consistent support.

Alice has always known that life is simplified if decisions are approached and carried out with an abiding faith. And perhaps life seemed simpler when she was a little girl skipping along Kialat Road, a place nearly as remote and unreachable today as it was when she was born.

Those who grow up in the embrace of the sea retain a lifelong bond to its timeless rhythms. It is the perfect metaphor for Alice's own life as well as for the life she shared with John, who always came to her by sea. For Alice, it had begun with the early morning boat rides she shared with her father to greet arriving ships from mysterious ports of call, or playing with her sister while flying a red kite along the sandy beach at Masu, with the wind chasing her and the waves pounding. For John, his early boyhood experiences on ships in the Caribbean and South America primed him for a life on the high seas that not only fulfilled a personal dream, but also saved the lives of thousands of men and women.

A love of the sea was so natural to both Alice and John that it became the unspoken passion of their union, linking past to future. As the admiral was always there for his sailors, Alice will keep them in her heart. Wherever the USS *Bulkeley* sails from her homeport of Norfolk, Virginia, the persevering spirit of the admiral and the gentler guiding spirit of his lady, Alice, will be near.

(Right) Alice Wood Bulkeley, November 19th, 1912–March 16th 2008.

Captain Peter Bulkeley, U.S. Navy, July 1989.

Shari, Tom and Tommy on board the USS B in Boston, March 3, 2003.

Joan Stade, USO Volunteer at deployments and welcome home ceremonies.

Tommy Hense, Tyler Krill, Samantha Krill, and Eric Hense with USO Care Packages, November 2007 Longboat Key, Florida

Appendix A

The Bulkeley Family

Hilda Alice Wood	Born Swatow, China	Nov. 19, 1912
John Duncan Bulkeley	Born New York City, NY	Aug. 19, 1911
	Died Silver Spring, MD	April 6, 1996
	Married	Nov. 10, 1938
	Shanghai, China	

Children of Alice Wood and John Bulkeley

Joan Bulkeley Stade	Born Oct. 1, 1940
John Duncan Bulkeley, Jr.	Born Apr. 3, 1942
Peter Wood Bulkeley	Born July 20, 1945
Regina Joy Bulkeley Day	Born Dec. 18, 1951
Diana Bulkeley Lindsay	Born Nov. 1, 1953

Grandchildren of Alice and John Bulkeley

To Joan Stade	Karen Elizabeth Stade Krill	Born Oct. 28, 1965
	Sharon Lynn Stade Hense	Born July 24, 1967
To Peter Bulkeley	Peter Tare Bulkeley	Born Mar. 22, 1979
		Died Sept. 11, 1981
	Lauren Leigh Bulkeley	Born Aug. 24, 1981
	Christopher Tare Bulkeley	Born Dec. 14, 1983
To Regina Day	John Raymond Day	Born Mar. 22, 1976
	Jennifer Lynn Day	Born July 6, 1977
To Diana Lindsay	Kelley Alice Lindsay	Born July 1, 1979
	Sharon Leigh Lindsay	Born Mar. 25, 1981

Appendix B

Vice Admiral John Bulkeley
Decorations and Campaigns

U.S. Decorations

Medal of Honor (presented by President Franklin D. Roosevelt)

Navy Cross (presented by Secretary of the Navy Frank Knox)

Distinguished Service Cross (Army) with Oak Leaf cluster in Lieu of Second Award (presented by Gen. Douglas MacArthur)

Distinguished Service Medal with two Gold Stars in Lieu of Second and Third Awards (presented by Chief of Naval Operations)

Silver Star (Army) with Gold Star in Lieu of a Second Award (Navy)

Legion of Merit with Combat Distinguishing Device - V - for Valor

Bronze Star with Gold Star in Lieu of a Second Award

Joint Services Commendations Medal

Purple Heart with Gold Star in Lieu of a Second Award

Army Distinguished Unit Award

U.S. Campaigns and Service Medals

China Service Medal - USS *Sacramento*

American Defense Service Medal with "Fleet" Clasp
American Campaign Medal

Asiatic-Pacific Campaign Medal with Three Bronze Battle Stars
for the following:
- Philippine Island Operations—1 Dec 1941 - 6 May 1942
- Eastern New Guinea Operations—Torpedo Boat Operations
  17 Dec 1942 - 24 Jul 1944
- Lae Occupation—4-22 Sept 1943

European-African-Middle East Campaign with Two Bronze Battle
Stars of the following:
- Invasion of Normandy
- Invasion of France

World War Two Victory Medal

National Defense Service Medal with Bronze Star for Second
Award

Korea Service Medal

Navy Expert Rifle Shot

Navy Expert Pistol Shot

Foreign Decorations and Service Awards
Philippine Distinguished Conduct Star (presented by President
Manuel Quezon of the the Republic of the Philippines)

Philippine Defense Service Medal

French Legion of Honor—Degree of Officer

French croix de guerre (presented by Gen. Charles de Gaulle;
Second Award presented by Monsieur Louis Mexandeau on
behalf of President François Mitterrand)

Korean Presidential Unit Citation

United Nations Korean Service Medal

Appendix C

Family Update

Alice Wood Bulkeley (b. 1912) currently lives in a retirement community in suburban Maryland. She continues to travel widely and her most recent trips have been on cruises in the Caribbean and the inland passage of Alaska. She attended the wedding of her granddaughter, Shari Stade, to Tom Hense on September 22, 2001, in Illinois. She sings in the church choir and belongs to many service clubs.

John Duncan Bulkeley (1911-1996) served in the U.S. Navy for fifty-eight years. His heroism and accomplishments have been well documented. He died on April 6, 1996, surrounded by his family, and is buried at Arlington National Cemetery.

Captain Cecil Herbert Wood (1880-1943) was born in London, England, and died March 26, 1943, while still a prisoner of war in Shanghai, China. Accounts of the circumstances of his death include that he was killed in attempting to escape with other prisoners.

Emily Ritsu Umetsu Wood (1889-1983) was born in Shimabara, a fishing village near Nagasaki, on the island of Kyushi, Japan. She lived to be ninety-four and died in Toronto, Ontario, Canada. Just the year before, at the age of ninety-three, she had climbed Centennial Hill, Etobicoke (near Toronto), for the Easter Sunday service that began with the first rays of the morning sun. She was a faithful member of the Anglican Church.

Joan Bulkeley Stade was born in 1940 in Long Beach, California. She attended the University of Maryland at College Park, Maryland, and the United Airlines Stewardess Training Center in Cheyenne, Wyoming. On December 21, 1962, she married **Herbert Arthur Stade** of Fairmont, Minnesota, a United Airlines pilot and land developer. They had met as passengers on a United DC-6 en route to Denver in the fall of 1961. **Karen Elizabeth,** who was named in honor of Joan's paternal grandmother, Elizabeth Bulkeley, arrived on October 28, 1965, and **Sharon Lynn** on July 24, 1967. On both of these occasions, Alice Bulkeley traveled from the naval base at Guantanamo Bay, Cuba, to assist with their care. Karen married **Scott Douglas Krill** on May 18, 1991. They have two children: **Samantha**

Alison, born January 2, 1997, and **Tyler Stade,** born January 27, 1999. Shari married **Thomas Craig Hense** on September 22, 2001, at Emmanuel Episcopal Church in La Grange, Illinois, where Joan and Herbert were married. Shari wore her mother's wedding dress. They are the parents of Tommy, Eric, and Emilia.

John Duncan Bulkeley Jr. was born in 1942 in Brooklyn, New York. Johnny became an organist at the Washington Navy Yard chapel, a post he held for twenty-two years. He now lives in his own condominium in the same retirement complex as Alic, in Silver Spring, Maryland.

Peter Wood Bulkeley, was born in 1945 in Brooklyn, New York. Following in his father's footsteps, he graduated from the U.S. Naval Academy in 1968, with Alice and Joan pinning on his ensign shoulder boards. He would go on to serve two tours in Vietnam, distinguishing himself as a combat-decorated veteran. In a crossed-sword ceremony at the Naval Academy Chapel, he married **Carol Ann Simmons** in 1977 and, early in their marriage, they lived overseas in Belgium, England, and Spain. During the Gulf War in 1991, Peter commanded the joint and combined British and U.S. Battleship and Mine Countermeasures Task Group, which conducted heavy bombardments of enemy positions to the south of Kuwait City. Peter and Carol are the parents of Lauren Leigh and Christopher Tare. They later divorced and Peter married Leikeim on April 24, 2008.

Regina (Gina) Joy Bulkeley Day was born in 1951, in Bethesda, Maryland. After finishing her education at Penn Hall, Radford College, and Florida Atlantic University, she became a registered nurse and special education teacher. Gina married Lt. (j.g.) Steven Day, USN, from Boynton Beach, Florida, on June 24, 1972, at the U.S. Naval Academy. They currently live in Alabama and have a son, John, and daughter, Jennifer.

Diana Bulkeley Lindsay was born in 1953, in Long Beach, California. She also attended Penn Hall, Radford College, and the University of Maryland. Diana married Harvey Lindsay, the "boy next door," from Silver Spring, Maryland, on October 14, 1978, at the Washington Navy Yard chapel, and stayed close to her parents in the Maryland area. They have two daughters. Diana and Harvey divorced in 2004 and she married Captain Terry Heuman USMC (Ret.) in 2005. They live in Rockville, Texas.

The Family in Australia

Edith Mary Hamson (b. 1911) celebrated her ninetieth birthday in July 2001. She currently lives with her daughter, May Thomson, in the lower Blue Mountains, southwest of Sydney.

Arthur Bird Hamson, Edith's husband, died November 18, 1975.

Mavis (May) Rosemary Hamson Thomson was born October 3, 1936, in Hong Kong. She married her cousin, George Madden, in 1955. He died tragically in 1957. May became a nurse and married Gordon Thomson, a sailor in the Merchant Navy. He died in December 2000. They raised two daughters and a son.

Richard Thorsbey Hamson was born December 19, 1938, in Hong Kong. He served in the Merchant Navy and is married to Beverly Langton. They reside in Mount Gambier and have two sons and a daughter. The family recently visited the United States and their American family.

Heather Rosalind Hamson was born February 21, 1950, and is married to Marvyn Raymond Browning. They have two sons and a daughter and four grandchildren. They live in Wagga Wagga.

Allana Thomson Arnoe Corbin, the youngest daughter of May Thomson, is a helicopter pilot and was the first woman to circumnavigate Australia solo in 1997 after a long, miraculous recovery from a 1990 plane crash. At the time of the crash, she was participating in a search-and-rescue mission. She was one of two survivors—six perished—and suffered a broken back and internal injuries. She taught herself to walk again and gained her commercial helicopter license. She works for the Tasmanian government as a helicopter rescue pilot. Allana is writing her second book, *Prisoners of the East,* to be published in 2002. (Her autobiography, *The Best I Can Be,* was published in 1998.) To research the current book, she and her parents visited Hong Kong and Swatow (now Shantou City), where they were saddened to discover that the family home on Masu (now Mayu) Island had been destroyed by fire and that the island today serves principally as a support for a four-lane bridge crossing the bay. Allana was of great assistance during the writing of *Twelve Handkerchiefs.* She lives in Otaga Bay, Tasmania with twin daughters.

The Family in Canada

Leilah Lois Wood was born December 28, 1928, in Swatow, China. She graduated from the Royal Conservatory in Toronto and taught private and group piano lessons for more than twenty-five years. She married her cousin, Morris Wood, a rancher. Leilah and Morris are both retired and live in

Saskatchewan, Canada. Leilah was of invaluable help with her knowledge of family history.

Eric Thorsby Wood was born February 21, 1915, in Masu, China. He worked as a civil engineer for thirty-seven years in Toronto. He and his wife, Marcie, are retired in Etobicoke, a Toronto suburb. Eric provided many details for *Twelve Handkerchiefs* from his recollections and personal papers.

In 1996, the three Wood sisters were reunited when Alice and Leilah flew to Australia to visit Edith. They spoke at length about their childhood and life experiences. Lending a sense of closure to their war years, Leilah returned to Edith the rag doll Edith had made for her during their imprisonment in Camp Stanley.

Appendix D

The origins of the handkerchief

From the Middle Ages through today, handkerchiefs have been exchanged as tokens of love between ladies and their courtiers. Long considered a proper gift for a lady to accept from a man, during the renaissance men pinned embroidered handkerchiefs to their sleeves—hence the expression "to wear one's heart upon one's sleeve"—or inside their hatbands. The word itself derives from the Old French word *covrechef*, indicating a covering (scarf) for the head or hands.

The traditions of Chinese embroidery reach back more than 4,000 years. Yue embroidery, from China's southeastern Guangdong province, features intricate patterns of flowers and fans embroidered with hair-thin thread. Yue embroidery has been highly prized by Europeans since the nineteenth century.

The handkerchiefs illustrated in this book all at one time belonged to Alice Wood Bulkeley and have been faithfully reproduced by Douglas Klauba, a Chicago-based artist, as the title pages for the twelve chapters. The current owners of these works of art, all of whom are daughters, granddaughters or great-granddaughters of Alice Bulkeley, are listed below:

Chapter 1: Shari Stade Hense
Chapter 2: Diana Bulkeley Lindsay
Chapter 3: Regina Bulkeley Day
Chapter 4: Jennifer Day
Chapter 5: Carol Simmons Bulkeley
Chapter 6: Joan Bulkeley Stade
Chapter 7: Samantha Krill
Chapter 8: Kelley Lindsay
Chapter 9: Lauren Bulkeley
Chapter 10: Shannon Lindsay
Chapter 11: Karen Krill
Chapter 12: Alice Wood Bulkeley

Select Bibliography

Books

Bachman, Bruce M. *An Honorable Profession: The Life And Times of One of America's Most Able Seamen: Rear Admiral John Duncan Bulkeley, USN.* New York: Vantage Press, 1985.

Breuer, William B., *Devil Boats: The PT War Against Japan.* Novato, Ca.: Presidio Press, 1987.

Breuer, William B. *Sea Wolf—The Daring Exploits of a Navy Legend, John D. Bulkeley.* Novato, Ca.: Presidio Press, 1989.

Copley, Helen F. *The Christy Quest.* Tucson, Ariz.: The Patrice Press, 1999.

White, W. L. *They Were Expendable.* Annapolis, Md.: Naval Institute Press, 1998. Published by arrangement with Harcourt Brace & Company. Originally published in 1942.

Periodicals, Videotape, Pamphlets

Boland, Susan. "The Port Pilot's Daughter," *Naval History,* Nov./Dec. 1998.

Coppola, Capt. Joseph A. USN (Ret.) "The Invasion of Swatow." *Shipmate,* April 1991.

Stade, Joan. "In Honor of Vice Admiral John D. Bulkeley, USN." (videotape compilation), 1994.

Stade, Joan. "In Tribute to Vice Admiral John D. Bulkeley, USN." (videotape compilation), 1996.

Stade, Sharon L. *Bulkeley Family Quotes & Collections,* 1996.

Interviews and Personal Collections

Arnot, Allana. Unpublished manuscript excerpts from *Prisoners of the East,* a book to be published by Pan-Macmillan, 2002.

Bulkeley, Alice Wood. Personal diaries, documents, correspondence and interviews from August 1999 - March 2001.

Bulkeley, Peter. Interviews and correspondence.

Cheung, Kittie. Interviews, correspondence, family documents.

Day, Regina Bulkeley. Interviews, correspondence, family documents.

Lindsay, Diana Bulkeley. Interviews, correspondence, family documents.

Rush, Sam and Lillian. Interviews, correspondence.

Wood, Eric. Interviews, correspondence, family documents.

Wood, Leilah. Interviews, correspondence.

BULKELEY FAMILY TREASURES

Joan Stade was born Joan Isabel Bulkeley on October 1, 1940, in Long Beach, California, the eldest of five children. Her father, John Duncan Bulkeley, and mother, Alice Wood Bulkeley, met and married in China during World War II when John was a junior officer on board a naval ship stationed along the coast near Hong Kong. Joan's father remained in the Navy, becoming an Admiral and moving the family around the country, including homes in New York, California, Maryland, Virginia, Tennessee and Washington, D.C. After attending the University of Maryland, Joan made a decision that would change her life. She became a stewardess for United Air Lines. On a flight to Wyoming for training, she met Herb Stade, a pilot who was headed to Denver for training. They married December 21, 1962, and settled in Oak Brook, Illinois, where they raised two daughters: Karen Elizabeth and Sharon Lynn. Today, Joan spends numerous hours volunteering on the board of the USO of Illinois and as a member of the Salvation Army Women's Auxiliary. She has also written several books about her family to preserve their legacy for future generations. Joan and Herb have traveled the world and still enjoy discovering new places. Her most precious time, however, is spent with her four grandchildren: Samantha, Tyler, Tommy and Eric.

This book is a gift and one can donate to The USO

of Illinois Navy pier at 700 East Grand Avenue, #105, Chicago, Illinois, 60611.

—•◦•—

My dear Mother,

Yesterday I had the greatest happiness in a long while, when I received your letter of 30th April. Edith's letter of June 1942 was also received earlier this year and I wrote several letters then. I do hope you will receive some of them before long. Yes, I have written at intervals ever since hostilities started. I am so glad Leilah is able to complete her education and that Eric is safe. Have had no word from him and cannot write him as I do not have his address. Am so glad you finally heard from Father. You probably know his troubles are over and you must not grieve. Just keep well and take care of yourselves. With the New year I wish for peace and a restoration to normal life. Am also pleased to hear Edith is using her artistic talents. Hope you all had as cheerful a Christmas as was possible. John and I are always thinking of you.

Joan and Johnny are fine and send love to you all. Johnny will be two in April. They are both blond and blue eyed. Loads of love to you all and keep your chins up.

Alice Wood Bulkeley

—•◦•—

4th October, 1943
Dear Alice,

Have written you nearly every month. No word from you yet. Two years since last heard from you. Hope you and family well. Thought of Joan on the 1st, Mavis's Birthday yesterday. Poor child, second birthday in camp. No presents. Had small party of little things we could make in camp. Mavis is seven now and growing tall. Love to you all. We are keeping well and cheerful.

Your loving sister,
Edith Hamson

COMMISSIONING OF USS *BULKELEY*

Gordon [England, Secretary of the Navy], thank you for that very warm introduction. Truly it's an honor for me to be able to be here today to represent President Bush and Secretary Rumsfeld at the commissioning of another great naval ship. Commander Del Toro, officers and members of the crew of the *Bulkeley,* many other distinguished guests that are here, including the veterans who join us today. And I'd like to extend a special welcome to those veterans for whom yesterday, December 7th, 60 years ago, marked the beginning of their wartime service. Also a very warm welcome to Alice Bulkeley and her family, who weathered over five decades of adventurous Navy life in war and in peace. We salute you all for your service to our country and we thank you for your role in sponsoring this mighty ship.

Mayor [of New York Rudolph] Giuliani, six months ago on Memorial Day, you and I stood just a few yards from this spot to pay tribute to the brave service of America's veterans. We were on the flight deck of *Intrepid,* a ship whose crew came through torpedo attacks and kamikaze attacks, proving that they were as intrepid as their ship was tough.

Since that Memorial Day, America has watched New York City come through its own Pearl Harbor. Like the sailors and Marines who served aboard *Intrepid,* New Yorkers have shown the world that they are not only tough, but intrepid as well. As the dictionary says, "outstandingly courageous, fearless." And New Yorkers have shown that behind that well-known veneer of toughness, there is an enormous capacity for compassion and caring for their fellow citizens.

It's often been said that tough times call for tough leaders, and Mr. Mayor, you have been tough and compassionate—traits that the world has now associated with New York. [Applause.]

I think it's a privilege for all of us to be here for the commissioning of a ship that will join our great Navy as an indispensable force for peace and freedom in the world. The USS *Bulkeley* deploys the most advanced weapon systems afloat today. She also demonstrates the power that only a free nation can generate. This newest Aegis destroyer is the product of the great partnership between government and industry that is crucial to the defense of our country and to peace and freedom in the world.

Not so long ago the ship behind me and her crew took part in the time-honored tradition of christening—conferring a name and a title on a structure of wood, rivets and steel, and establishing a partnership with those who will sail her into harm's way.

Over the past couple of years, since the christening, the men and women of the *Bulkeley* have strengthened this partnership with their sweat and their meticulous care, guiding their ship through her first sea trials, taking her from a concept to a living, breathing ship of the fleet.

Today as the commissioning crew of the *Bulkeley*, the crew will acquire the distinguished naval title of "plank owner"—a tradition going back to the days of the wooden sailing ships.

The commissioning crew of the *Bulkeley* will retain those honors and prestige throughout their lives and each plank owner is owed a clear, free, open and unencumbered title to one plank of the deck upon the ship's decommissioning.

Indeed, for the first crew of the *Bulkeley*, this is your day and we salute you. [Applause.]

New York City is known for its creativity, for being on the cutting edge of innovation. And New Yorkers have long been known for their toughness. And in recent days the world has seen the bravery of New Yorkers and the concern for their fellow citizens.

There is no more fitting place to commission this ship, here within the shadow of Lady Liberty and within walking distance of Ground Zero. In doing so, we honor the tough old Sea Wolf who repeatedly showed throughout his career that he was not afraid to stand up to anyone who threatened our freedom.

Through a career that spanned more than five decades of active duty service, John Bulkeley was tough in standing up for his Navy and his nation. His exploits made him a living legend.

In the first weeks of World War II with most of the Pacific fleet wiped out and nothing but bad news coming from the Pacific, Lieutenant Bulkeley and his men changed all that when they sank a Japanese cruiser. And they kept up the fight. With little or no spare parts, ammunition or food, their motor torpedo boats repeatedly and unhesitatingly attacked Japanese ships in the Philippines, sustaining their operations for four months and seven days with almost no support except their own ingenuity and daring.

With Corregidor under siege and Japanese forces closing in, Bulkeley's PT boats spirited General of the Army Douglas MacArthur and the President of the Philippines through 600 miles of seas infested with enemy warships. By MacArthur's own reckoning, they snatched the commander of U.S. forces "out of the jaws of death."

That heroic action in the Pacific earned the young sailor the Congressional Medal of Honor, the admiration of our nation, and a ticker tape parade here in his hometown, right down Broadway. A crowd of more than a million people turned out to honor Lieutenant Bulkeley and his crew. And while here it may not surprise you, a theatrical agent smelling something approached Bulkeley to see if he would be interested in making stage appearances in theater here. Big money in it, he told Bulkeley. But the young hero told the agent that the only theater he was interested in playing was the theater in Tokyo.

However, Commander Bulkeley did go on to play another theater, the European Theater, commanding a destroyer named *Endicott*. A month after D-Day, with only one of Endicott's guns working, he attacked two German corvettes at point blank range and sank them both. Afterwards he said, "As long as we had even one gun left I was going to attack. That's what's expected of a United States Navy officer and warship."

When America faced a growing crisis in this hemisphere, Admiral Bulkeley took that same toughness to Cuba in 1963 to command Guantanamo Naval Base and face off with Fidel Castro. He cut the water line that Castro had turned off and vowed that we would never again depend on Cuba as a water source. To this day, we don't.

Like a lot of other New Yorkers, though, Admiral Bulkeley's toughness was matched by his caring for the people in his community—his sailors and his Marines. From his early backbreaking days aboard a coal-burning ship in China, he had learned that improving the safety and overall running of a ship saves lives. Through 21 years of service as head of the Navy's Board of Inspection and Survey, Admiral Bulkeley attacked the job of ensuring that our ships were fit for combat with the same fervor that he had shown in combat.

There is no doubt that this man helped save countless lives. It is a legacy that extends to the sailors and Marines who will man the *Bulkeley* today.

And as John Bulkeley was tough and caring, he was also innovative. As is so often the case, innovation is not just about new technology. It is about using old things in new ways that have new and dramatic impacts. We see that in Afghanistan today where brave members of our Special Forces literally mounted on horseback have combined 50-year-old B-52 bombers with 19th Century horse cavalry to create a truly 21st Century military capability.

John Bulkeley had that same ability to solve problems and innovate new solutions, a trait he relied on from the very start of his naval career.

He had always wanted to attend the Naval Academy but all the appointments in his district were gone, so he had to find some other way to get there. The Bulkeley family owned some land in Texas, so young John went to Washington and found the congressman from that district in Texas and talked him into an appointment from the Lone Star State. Problem solved. The Texan from New York was on his way.

In the Philippines, he and the men in his PT boat squadron fought on despite a lack of spare parts, repair facilities and fuel—making things work by clever innovation. His Medal of Honor citation notes not only his daring and his gallantry, but also his unique resourcefulness and ingenuity.

When he was in charge of the Navy's Board of Inspections and Survey, his solution to significant problems that could affect the fleet was an invention that came to be known as "Dear John" letters that he sent to a mailing list that included most of the senior Navy leadership. Those letters ended with the phrase, "just thought you'd like to know about this," and they became legendary for getting the job done.

In one example, John Bulkeley insisted that emergency escape breathing devices be installed on every ship in the fleet. Good idea, but too expensive, he was told. But he didn't quit. He fought to get them. And as usually happened when John Bulkeley fought for something, he won. Those devices were put on every ship and he lived to see the difference it made when the USS *Stark,* the frigate, came under Iraqi missile attack in the Persian Gulf in 1987. Thirty-seven sailors perished in that tragedy, but many more would have died from the smoke and flames were it not for the breathing devices that John Bulkeley had put on board.

The motto of this new ship is "Freedom's Torch." John Duncan Bulkeley carried freedom's torch with honor and made the Navy better for generations to come.

The generation that now takes up freedom's torch takes our story full circle. Carlos Del Toro left communist Cuba as a child, came to this country, attended the Naval Academy and rose through the ranks to take command of the Navy's newest destroyer. That story is in itself a testament to the promise of our nation and to Carlos Del Toro's own tough fighting spirit. And it probably didn't hurt that, like John Bulkeley himself, Carlos Del Toro grew up in New York City. [Applause.]

I'll conclude by mentioning one other distinguished New Yorker, a former President and a former Assistant Secretary of the Navy, by the way, Teddy Roosevelt, who once captured why it is so important for our country to maintain our armed forces as second to none. He said, "We Americans have many grave problems to solve, many threatening evils to fight, and many deeds to do if, as we hope and believe, we have the wisdom, the strength, the courage and the virtue to do them. But we must face facts as they are. Our nation," he said 100 years ago, "is the one among all nations of the earth which holds in its hands the fate of the coming years."

That was true in Teddy Roosevelt's time, it was true on December 7, 1941, it was true on September 11, 2001, and it will be true throughout the service of the proud ship we are commissioning today.

I would like to thank all of you who have made the *Bulkeley* live and breathe. Like the man for whom she is named, like the men and women in uniform serving our nation so faithfully and so nobly today, this ship will be a force for peace and freedom.

May God bless this ship, may God bless her crew, may God bless our great Navy, and may God bless America. [Applause.]

Fortunately, before she passed away, she was able to see the ship named for her husband just one more time, being awarded the Arizona Award for excellence, last year in 2007. Dressed in her 'uniformed' blouse and USS *Bulkeley* commissioning hat, brought good memories of a Navy wife and a lady who loved our Navy and her husband to no end. She was so proud, lived a very long life and was so involved in so many ways with the Navy and its men and women who serve.

Captain Peter Wood Bulkeley, USN (Ret.)
March 31, 2008
From a letter to Admiral Jonathan Greenert

BULKELEY RECOGNIZED AS TOP
IN COMBAT READINESS

Navy NewsStand
Story Number: NNS070725-09
Release Date: 7/25/2007 1:28:00 PM
By: Mass Communication Specialist 1st Class (SW) Stefanie
Holzeisen-Mullen, Fleet Public Affairs Center Atlantic

NORFOLK (NNS)—Chief of Naval Operations Adm. Mike
Mullen announced the guided-missile destroyer USS *Bulkeley*
(DDG 84) as the winner of the calendar year 2005 and 2006
USS *Arizona* Memorial Trophy Winner in a message deliv-
ered to the fleet July 12.

Established in 1995, the award is presented to the ship
demonstrating the greatest combat readiness in strike warfare, surface-fire support, anti-terrorism and force protection,
and anti-surface warfare during a two-year competitive cycle.

"The Arizona Trophy is a real source of pride for us,
especially when viewed against the overall level of incredible
readiness throughout the fleet," said Cmdr. John Beaver,
Bulkeley's commanding officer. "The title of Vice Admiral
(John) Bulkeley's biography is 'Seawolf' and within the life-
lines of the ship we refer to ourselves as 'The Wolfpack.'
To have earned this award means we have been true to the
admiral's direction."

Bulkeley served as force track coordinator and sea combat commander for the Iwo Jima Expeditionary Strike Group
(ESG) during their 2006 deployment.

While operating in the U.S. 5th Fleet area of responsibility, *Bulkeley* served as overall air warfare commander for the
ESG, leading coalition forces in interdicting illicit maritime
and terrorist activities while conducting maritime interdic-
tion operations. Their leadership help set conditions for

security and stability and complemented the counter-terrorism and security efforts of regional nations.

"All of our success is a result of a relentless training program and the motivated Sailors who serve day-in, day-out," said Fire Controlman 2nd Class (SW) Jeffery Lewetzki, workcenter supervisor for the Aegis computer suite in *Bulkeley*'s Combat Systems Fire Control Division and a member of the ship's visit, board, search and seizure (VBSS) team. "Since I first checked onboard, the crew has always had a 'one team, one fight' mentality which has contributed to our success as a ship in all mission areas."

"I am honored this great warship, named after a great American hero, has received this award," said Electronics Technician 1st Class (SW/AW) Dave Jackel, Combat Systems Elctronic Materials Division leading petty officer and team leader on the "Wolfpack" VBSS team. "The name Bulkeley has meant great things throughout the course of naval history and we intend to continue that tradition into the future."

According to Beaver, the award belongs to the more than 450 Sailors and two commanding officers who served on board in the last two years, working together to function as a cohesive unit to deny foreign enemies the ability to use the sea as a safe haven.

"There is no magic formula for superior readiness, it only comes from work. It's the tenacity and ingenuity of the Sailors on the deckplates and the hard-won trust and confidence they have in the command leadership that has been the difference for us," said Beaver. "Every ship out there is working hard and when we accept this award, we will do so on behalf of all the Sailors who do the right thing watch after watch."

Admiral John Bulkeley was a patriot, a legend, and a hero in the truest sense. A husband and a father, he was a simple man who did his duty as God gave him the ability to do it, a man who tried to keep a low profile but somehow always ended up in the limelight of life. He devoted his entire life to his country and to his Navy. Six decades of his life were spent in the active defense of America. Even after retirement in 1988, he remained engaged in the direction of our Navy and our country. He represented the U.S. Navy and veterans at Normandy during D-Day celebrations, laying wreaths and flowers at the graves of his and our fallen comrades; he provided inspirational speeches to our youth and to our leadership. He believed in America; he believed in a strong defense; he believed in a Navy he loved more than his own life.

John Bulkeley's destiny may have been cast long before he sought the salt spray of the open ocean. His ancestors, including Richard Bulkeley, brought aboard HMS VICTORY by Lord Nelson just prior to the Battle of Trafalgar in 1804; John Bulkeley of HMS WAGER under Captain Bligh, who sailed with Anson's Squadron to raid Spanish silver ships of the new world; and Charles Bulkeley, raising the Union Jack for the first time on an American warship, the ALFRED, commanded by John Paul Jones, influenced his intense love of the sea. He was born in New York City, grew up on a farm in Hacketstown, NJ, and wrote his high school class poem in 1928, if you can believe that. He loved opera. He loved animals and took great care of feeding and caring for any that sought his help. He was compassionate to their needs. He loved his black cat.

His love of the sea, however, was his dream and his destiny. Unable to gain an appointment to Annapolis from his home state of New Jersey, he was led by his determination to Washington, and, after knocking on a lot of doors, he gained an appointment from the state of Texas. As America dealt with the Great Depression, his dream of going to sea, however, received a set back. Only half of the 1933 Academy class that graduated received a commission. John Bulkeley, noted early on for his intense interest in engineering, went on and joined the Army Flying Corps. Like the crazy flying machines of the day, he landed hard more than once and, after a year, left flying for the deck of a cruiser, the INDIANAPOLIS, as a commissioned officer in the United States Navy.

Ensign John D. Bulkeley charted an interesting course in his early years and was recognized early on by the Navy's leadership. As a new ensign in the mid-thirties, he took the initiative to remove the Japanese ambassador's brief case from a stateroom aboard a Washington-bound steamer, delivering same to Naval Intelligence a short swim later. This bold feat, of which there were to be many more in his life, didn't earn him any medals, but it did get him a swift one way ticket out of the country and a new assignment as Chief Engineer of a coal burning gunboat, the SACRAMENTO, also known in those parts as "The Galloping Ghost of the China Coast." Picture in your minds the movie "Sand Pebbles." There he was to meet a young, attractive English girl at a dinner party aboard HMS DIANA. Alice Wood and the handsome swashbuckling John Bulkeley would, in the short period of courtship, live an incredible story together. In China they would witness the invasion of Swatow and Shanghai by Japanese troops and the bombing of the *Panay*. They were strafed by warring planes and watched from a hotel soldiers at war in the street below. John Bulkeley, with an uncanny propensity to stir things up, often took the opportunity to bait the occupying Japanese soldiers, dashing with his bride to be into no-mans land, chased by Japanese soldiers, and, every once in awhile, shooting them with an air pistol on their backsides "just for fun." He fit the mold of Indiana Jones, hat, coat, and all, and not necessarily a commissioned officer in fore and aft cap of the day.

John Bulkeley learned a lot from his experience as a Chief Engineer and also what war was all about and what an enemy invading force was capable of doing. At the dawn of World War II, and now a fleet lieutenant commanding motor torpedo boats, John Bulkeley hit his stride as a daring, resourceful and courageous leader, determined to fight to the last against enemy forces attacking the Philippine Islands. His exploits are what make legends as well as movies. As a young lieutenant he would say, "No one knows what war is about until you're in it." Fearless in battle, resourceful, and daring was John Bulkeley. Men like George Cox, skipper of PT41, would write in 1943, "I would follow this man to Hell if asked." A lot of others would agree. General of the Army Douglas MacArthur, after being ordered out of the Philippines and arriving at Mindanao following a 600 mile open ocean escape aboard a 77-foot motor torpedo boat through enemy lines, would say, "You have taken me out of the jaws of death. I shall never forget it."

John Bulkeley's daring exploits will never be forgotten. Hard as leather on the outside, he was also a man with compassion and love for his fellow man. Reflecting upon those terrible early days of World War II, he wept over the decision that his men and our Army at Bataan were left behind to face an enemy of overwhelming strength, but he also acknowledged that when the coach calls upon you to bunt and sacrifice, you do, with all the strength and conviction you can muster, for the overall victory cannot be achieved unless we are prepared to give it our all. From the Pacific campaign, where he would command another squadron of PTs, he would go to the European theater just in time for the Normandy invasion. At Charles de Gaulle Airport, a WWII vet, recognizing the Admiral, engaged him in a conversation. As they departed, the Admiral said to this vet, "See you in the next war." Upon hearing this, the veteran quickly came to attention, rendered a snappy salute, and responded, "I'll be there, ready to fight."

Where do we find such men? John Bulkeley led naval forces of torpedo boats and minesweepers in clearing the lanes to Utah Beach, keeping German E-Boats from attacking the landing ships along the Mason Line and picking up wounded sailors from the sinking minesweeper TIDE and destroyer CORY. The tale of his WWII exploits would not be complete without the mention of his love for destroyers, of which he would command many in his years to come. As Normandy operations wound up, he got his first large ship command, the destroyer ENDICOTT, and a month after the D-day invasion of Europe he came to the aid of two British gunboats under attack by two German corvettes. Charging in as dawn's light broke the horizon with his uncanny ability and determined leadership, with only one gun working, but with a band of brothers for a crew, he unhesitantly engaged both enemy vessels at point blank range, sending both to the bottom. When I asked him about this action, he replied, "What else could I do? You engage, you fight, you win. That is the reputation of our Navy, then and in the future."

The Admiral was a strong believer in standards, some would say, from the old school, as the enemy Captain of one of the corvettes soon learned. Coming up from the sea ladder, he would not salute the colors of the ENDICOTT, and was promptly tossed back into the sea. The third time did the trick, and he was taken prisoner and allowed on deck. World War II closed, and the Admiral emerged as one of the Navy's and America's most decorated heroes, having been awarded the Medal of Honor, the Navy Cross, the Army Distinguished Service Cross with Oak Leaf Cluster in lieu of a second award, two Silver Stars, the Legion of Merit with Combat V, the Purple Heart twice over, the Philippine Distinguished Conduct Star, and from France, the French Croix de Guerre. Asked about his many decorations, John Bulkeley would only comment, "Medals and awards don't mean anything. It's what's inside you, how you feel about yourself, that counts."

With an eye to the future, John Bulkeley looked forward to the day he would become an admiral in the navy he loved so much. As President Kennedy in the early months of his administration dealt with an ever-increasing crisis over Cuba, the Admiral got his wish and for a quarter of a century would serve as a flag officer in the Navy. Challenged in his first assignment as Commander, Guantanamo Naval Base, he met and defeated the challenge of Fidel Castro's threats of severing the water supplies of the base. Today, Guantanamo stands as a symbol of American resolve because men like John Bulkeley stood up, refused to bend, and took the initiative to stare down belligerent threats of lesser men not friendly with America. Perhaps a tribute of the time was the wanted poster, offering 50,000 pesos for him, dead or alive, by the communist leadership of Cuba along with a description, "...a guerrilla of the worst species." At Guantanamo, as those that have visited know, there is a hill that overlooks the northeast gate, A Gate, with a sign that reads "Cuba, Land Free from America." As Cuban troops began moving about, his 19-year-old-driver, a Marine lance corporal, came running up and stood directly in front of the Admiral, ready and willing to take the bullet that would end the life of his Commander. The Admiral loved his Marines; the Marines loved and respected him in return. He would be with them day and night, in fatigues, ready to conduct war if necessary but more to defend Americans and The Land of the Free against the communist yoke of tyranny. As COL Stevens, the former commanding officer of the Marine barracks at Guantanamo, wrote, adding three more stories to the legend of John Bulkeley, "The Admiral had the compassion for the men in the field, taking time again and again to bring them relief, whether cookies on Christmas morning or visiting them at odd hours of the night to ease their nerves. They loved this man." The Admiral would construct on that hill the largest Marine Corps insignia in the world as a quiet reminder that the United States Marine Corps stood vigilance over the base. In tribute, a Marine would write, "John Bulkeley, Marine in Sailor's clothing."

John Bulkeley never forgot his early years, the hard-iron like discipline, the poor material condition of the fleet, and the need to always be ready, in his own words, "...to be able to conduct prompt, sustained, combat operations at sea." Assigned as President of the Board of Inspection and Survey, a post held by many distinguished naval officers since its inception almost at the beginning of the Navy, his boundless energy would take him aboard every ship in the Navy, from keel to top of the mast, from fire control system to inside a boiler, discussing readiness and sharing sea stories and a cup of coffee with the men who operate our ships, planes, and submarines. He was relentless in his quest to improve the safety and material condition of the fleet and the conditions for the health and well being of those that manned them. He conducted his inspections by the book in strict accordance with standards as many a man well knows, but his love for the sailors always came through. His "Just thought you'd like to know" letters were another invention of his that were designed to be "unofficial reports" but of course were often greeted by a groan from the recipient in the Navy's leadership, knowing that John Bulkeley had another concern that needed attention and that the list of information addressees receiving the same "Just thought you'd like to know" letter often was longer than the letter itself. The Admiral would laugh about his informal invention.

After fifty-five years of commissioned service, John Bulkeley retired to private life. John Bulkeley did not like notoriety and wanted to keep a low profile throughout his life, even on his last day in the Navy. His ceremony, as requested, was brief and to the point, held in the CNO's office, with family present. All he sought after giving his entire life to his country and his service was to have the CNO's Flag Lieutenant open the door so he could slip his mooring line and leave quietly. John Bulkeley's career and service to the nation spanned six turbulent decades of the 20th century. He saw first hand desperate times and the horror of war. Yet he was also a father, marrying the woman he loved, and in his own words, "It was the best thing I ever did." He raised a family he could be proud of. His wife was his right arm, his closest friend for a long and full life. She gave him love and support. She was truly "The Wind Beneath His Wings." Before he passed away, his family, every member, child, grandchild, son, and daughter-in-law came to be with him in his last days. This by itself is testimony to the legacy he left behind and the love his family had for him. Admiral Bulkeley's efforts and sacrifices for a better world, a free world, his integrity and honor, and a combat ready fleet, ready to conduct prompt, sustained combat operations are his legacy to our nation.

Paraphrased from eulogy for Admiral John D. Bulkeley presented by his son:

Captain Peter W. Bulkeley
19 April 1996
Ft Myer Memorial Chapel
Arlington National Cemetery

(20.)

45-12 41st Street.
Sunnyside, New York.
April 23rd 1942!

My Darling.

There is no need for me to
be congratulating you, as I always knew you could
do it. Another cruiser, so I am told. You have done
wonders with those PT boats, and most certainly have put
them on the map. But as always my one concern is
that you are safe, and somehow you know this and have
been so thoughtful in sending me messages from time to
time. And so you can imagine how relieved I was to
receive your cable stating that you were safe and in
Australia. Darling, I do wish you could come home, for
a while anyway. Knowing you so well, I realize it
would take a good deal to make you leave your job.

The U.S. public think you are just
wonderful, and consequently demands have been made of
your mother and myself to make appearances etc to
bolster the morale of the women. It is a difficult role
for me, and one that you can easily understand I do
not relish at all. And your little son too, must
make his bow to the public, poor darling. Enclosed is
one of the many shots taken of us. And enlarged picture
is being sent you by clipper. Hope you like it, Darling.
Since my absence from home, Joan has become a
little out of hand, though she is just a healthy rascal.

I shall have to start in on her soon. This time I have recovered very quickly and am able to do almost anything already!

In fact Darling, I am hoping, you will be hearing me speak over the radio on Sunday night — April 2. It is the "We the People" program over WABC, and apparently the War Department has sanctioned it, and will let you know of it by cable. For a social climber there are opportunities galore, but all I want is, you home and some peace. Today the Paramount newsreel people were round again, to make a film of me, telling my side of the story, but I had to turn it down, as I just could not go through with it. Your mother thinks the experiences offered me are worth taking and on the whole I am doing pretty well. You are in the spotlight now, and as you have never failed me, so I am trying not to fail you.

Your mother works very hard these days, and now I hope to relieve her. It isn't easy for her any more and she really has been wonderful to me. Aunt Isabel is back on a cruise and the same as ever. Jasper is fine - also Bunky. Joan is now feeding herself and "Dada" is still constantly on her lips. Like everyone else she hears a great deal about her wonderful Daddy. It would be nice if she could really know you. And now Darling I must close. We all love you so much and hope to see you soon. Please take good care of yourself.

Always, ever
your lovingly
Alice

MEMORIAL AWARD

Ronald L. Friske
Memorial Award

The Ronald L. Friske Memorial Award is presented annually by the USO of Illinois in deep appreciation to a person who has provided outstanding service and support to those the USO serves: the men, women and families of the Armed Forces.

The award is presented in honor and memory of Ronald L. Friske, a long time Director and Treasurer of the USO of Illinois; who served in numerous positions including Chairman of the Finance Committee.

The first award was presented in 1995 to Colonel Arthur W. Gustafson, USA (Ret).

The USO is proud and honored to welcome the Friske family here tonight.

★ ★ ★ ★ ★

Mrs. Ronald L. Friske & the President and Board of Directors of the USO of Illinois are proud to present the 2002 Ronald L Friske Memorial Award to

JOAN BULKELEY STADE

Joan has served on the Board of Directors of the USO of Illinois for 6 years. Volunteer, author, wife, daughter, mother and grandmother... no matter what, Joan dedicates her time, talent, vision and heart.

We Salute You!

★ 9 ★

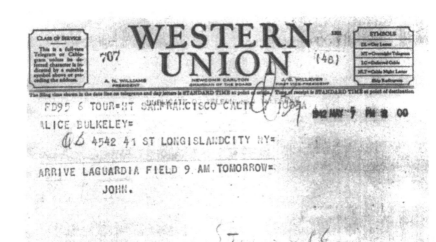

FD95 6 TOUR=NT SANFRANCISCO CALIF 1942A

LICE BULKELEY=

4542 41 ST LONGISLANDCITY NY=

ARRIVE LAGUARDIA FIELD 9 AM TOMORROW=

JOHN.

1942 MAY 7 PM 2 00

WESTERN UNION (30)

NC184VIA RCA=F AUSTRALIA 16 NFD   1942 APR 23 PM 4 33

LC MRS JOHN D BULKELEY=

4542 41ST STREET LONGISLANDCITY NY=

SAFE AND WELL IN AUSTRALIA=

JOHN BULKELEY.

Mrs. Douglas MacArthur
Waldorf Astoria Towers
New York, New York 10022

                              January 13, 1987

Dear John,

I want to say how very pleased I am at the well
deserved honor you are receiving today. Tnose
of us on those frail PTboats on tnose fateful
days in March of 1942, owe our lives to your
leadership and skill in running the Japanese
blockade. The success of that mission changed
the course of the war and the course of history.
"My General" would be proud of you today.

Please accept all of my love on this happy
occasion.

                    Fondly,

                    Jean MacArthur

Index

United Service Organizations of Illinois, Inc.
★ Chicago ★ Midway ★ Naval Training Center Great Lakes ★ O'Hare ★

August 2001

When the USO was established by President Franklin Delano Roosevelt in 1941, the mission was declared to be "in times of peace and war, to enhance the quality of life of the men and women of the Armed Forces and their families through social, spiritual, recreational and entertainment services". Sixty years later, this mission continues as millions of our country's dedicated and selfless military enjoy the "touch of home" provided by USO volunteers and staff all over the world.

The ultimate patriotism of Admiral Bulkeley is carried out today through the unselfish works of his daughter, Joan, as she tirelessly strives to better the lives of today's military. As a volunteer with the USO, Joan along with hundreds of other caring individuals, give of their time, their ideas, their experience and their resources to ensure that those who sacrifice their lives every day to protect our freedom are well cared for by the USO.

The USO of today has adapted to the changing needs of today's military, providing family outreach programs, internet and e-mail, game rooms and libraries, holiday dinners and, always, refreshments and conversation. As the members of the Armed Forces and their families continue to dedicate their lives to safeguarding our nation, the USO is always there to "serve those who serve" as we proudly act as "home away from home" wherever they may be.

Jan Emmert
President
USO of Illinois, Inc.

Totally supported by private contributions.
The mission of the USO of Illinois, in times of peace and war, is to enhance the quality of life of the men and women of the Armed Forces and their families through social, spiritual, recreational and entertainment services.

USO of IL Main Office 200 N. Michigan Ave., Suite 604, Chicago, IL 60601
Phone (312) 781-0730 ★ Fax (312) 781-0740 ★ E-Mail usoofil@interaccess.com ★ Website www.uso.org